The Random House Practice Book for Writers

The Random House Practice Book for Writers

Michael Hennessy
John Carroll University

Random House
New York

Acknowledgments

p. 26: From Les Thornburg, "Eyes," *International Wildlife,* p. 6. Copyright 1983, National Wildlife Federation. Reprinted from the September–October 1983 issue of INTERNATIONAL WILDLIFE.

pp. 30–31: From "For Many Germans, It's *Cool* to *Import* Words from English: *Jeans, Love,* and *Diversifikation,*" by Wanda Menke-Gluckert, *The Chronicle of Higher Education,* March 18, 1987, p. 53. Copyright 1987: The Chronicle of Higher Education. Reprinted with permission.

Preface

The Random House Practice Book for Writers is a collection of some 250 exercises designed to accompany *The Random House Handbook,* Fifth Edition, by Frederick Crews. While the *Practice Book* offers help for students who need to review basics, it also stresses rhetorical effectiveness, with full coverage of the larger elements of composition, from prewriting to revising, from considering audience and purpose to using prose strategies. The book provides ample material for class discussion and group work, as well as individual instruction.

The *Practice Book* has a number of distinctive features:

- *It takes a positive approach to writing.* Students learn to correct errors, but they also learn to use language effectively. The chapter on the sentence, for example, puts as much emphasis on constructing strong sentences as it does on revising weak ones.
- *It emphasizes editing practice, not drill.* The exercises on usage, punctuation, and mechanics are full and complete, but whenever possible, such exercises place error in context, asking students to edit sentences and paragraphs rather than to fill in blanks.
- *It engages student interest with colorful, informative writing.* The subject matter of the exercises comes from a wide range of published sources—

speeches, newspapers, popular magazines, academic journals, historical documents, short stories, and novels. Students study diction in the United States Constitution, parallelism in a speech by John F. Kennedy, and paragraph coherence in a passage by Eudora Welty. They read about mermaids, cucumbers, elephants, and computers; about colonial women and Viking warriors; about theories of language and styles of dress.

- *It includes many examples of student writing.* More than fifty samples of student writing illustrate prose strategies, sentence and paragraph construction, and essay development. There are six full essays, one of them a research paper. (An asterisk at the end of a passage indicates student writing.)

The *Practice Book* is divided into seven parts. The first part introduces various prose strategies, illustrating them with models and asking students to practice the strategies in their own writing. In the second part, students will find a step-by-step guide for writing an essay, including full coverage of draft writing and revision. Part III gives further practice in revision, emphasizing the shaping of effective paragraphs and sentences and the selection of precise, lively words. The next three parts (IV–VI) cover the nuts-and-bolts of writing: usage, punctuation, and conventions. As elsewhere in the book, the emphasis is on revision and editing. The book ends with a section on the research essay.

The exercises in the *Practice Book* are keyed to various parts of *The Random House Handbook*. The first exercise, for example, refers students to section 1a of the *Handbook*. This system of cross references encourages students to use the *Handbook* as a reference tool. An Answer Key for the *Practice Book* is available on request from Random House.

I owe special thanks to Frederick Crews for suggesting this book in the first place and for giving his enthusiastic support to its predecessor, *The Borzoi Practice Book for Writers.* At Random House, Steve Pensinger, Jeannine Ciliotta, and especially David Morris attended patiently and with good humor to a host of details, especially in the final stages of the project. I am also grateful to Pat Deduck, Lee Mellick, Chris McElyea, and Dan Lochman for providing examples from their students' prose; to my students at Southwest Texas State University for allowing me to reprint, and often adapt, their writing; and to Kelli Bavousette for helping me assemble the manuscript. Finally, I wish to thank my family—Susie, Nora, Kevin, and Bridget—for their many contributions to the book.

Michael Hennessy

Contents

The
Random House
Practice Book
for Writers

1

EXPLORING PROSE STRATEGIES

1
Strategies of Description and Narration

DESCRIPTION

1–1 Sharpening Your Powers of Observation (*RHH,* 1a)

Vivid descriptive writing often begins with careful observation of the physical world. Find a place that interests you—a park, a beach, a crowded shopping mall, a cluttered kitchen—and spend some time there observing and recording details. Try not to limit yourself to things you see; use your ears, nose, and skin as well as your eyes. Record the details below.

Place Observed: _____

Details:

_____

_____

3

_____

_____

_____

_____

_____

_____

_____

_____

_____

_____

_____

_____

_____

1–2 Using Details to Build a Descriptive Paragraph (*RHH,* 1a–1b)

Review the details you gathered for Exercise 1-1. Then write a paragraph describing the place you observed. Start the paragraph with a general statement that summarizes your overall impression of the place; then supply concrete, specific details to flesh out that impression. Use your own paper.

1–3 Using Concrete, Specific Language (*RHH,* 1a)

Expand the following sentences by using concrete, specific language to sharpen their descriptive power.

Example: The ashtray was full.

> *Standing among empty glasses,
> bottles, and Coke cans, the
> yellow ashtray overflowed with a
> week's worth of stale cigarette*

4

butts and discarded gum wrappers.

1. The lawn was well groomed.

2. The air felt very cold.

3. The snack was delicious.

4. Paul's kitchen smelled wonderful.

5. Julia's face looked strained.

1–4 Establishing a Descriptive Point of View— Physical Perspective (*RHH*, 1b)

Write two paragraphs in which you describe the same person, animal, object, or scene from drastically different physical vantage points. Use your imagination. Example: a child's view of an adult, first looking up from the floor, then face-to-face after the adult picks the child up. Use your own paper.

1–5 Establishing a Descriptive Point of View— Attitude (*RHH*, 1b)

Choose one of the following topics or a topic of your own, and write two descriptive paragraphs, one indicating a favorable attitude towards the subject, the other an unfavorable attitude. Instead of directly telling the reader your attitude, use descriptive details that show how you feel. Be prepared to discuss the kind of detail you selected for each paragraph. Use your own paper.

1. A thunderstorm
2. A ride in a speeding car
3. A desert landscape
4. An actor's face
5. A weightlifter's body

1–6 Using a Characteristic Action to Describe (*RHH*, 1c)

We recognize animals most obviously by the way they look, but we also associate certain actions or mannerisms with many animals, actions that reveal the animal's "personality"—a kitten playing with a string; an elephant swaying rhythmically from side to side, the top of its trunk brushing the ground; a bat swooping and dipping in the night air. Using the following paragraph as a model, describe an animal, revealing its "personality" through characteristic actions. Use your own paper.

MODEL PARAGRAPH

Two of the most appealing characteristics of *Lutra canadensis* are its playfulness and the fact that it is easily tamed and shows no great fear of humans. During the winter

6

otters often come up quite near to us to feed and play, and I have seen them cavorting alone or with their families. Their legs tucked safely at their sides, they take turns sliding down a slope leaving a long shallow groove in the snow. In the summer they slip down smooth clay banks well lubricated by the water, playing like children.[1]

Note: The next three exercises illustrate the use of figurative language in descriptive writing. For additional practice with figurative language, see Exercise 8–20, page 183.

1–7 Recognizing Figurative Language in Descriptive Writing (*RHH,* 1d)

Underline the figurative language in the following passages. Be prepared to discuss how the writer's use of such language contributes to the description. How would each passage differ if the writer had used no figurative language? Note any other features that make the passage vivid.

1. I was walking by the Thames. Half-past morning on an autumn day. Sun in a mist. Like an orange in a fried fish shop.[2]

2. During a spring rain, the attic was a place of wonder. My sister and I would climb the steep pull-down stairs just to hear the rain dancing on the tin roof. At one end of the room we could see the wind-tossed tree tops licking against the window panes. And when the wind blew up, it whistled merrily under the eaves.*

3. From the far side of the room, his face looked like the soft, drooping face of a bloodhound. The cheeks sagged heavily under their own weight. The eyes were buried under folds of loose skin. But up close, his face became an intricate roadmap, highways cutting across his forehead, tiny backroads branching out from the corners of his mouth and eyes and twisting their way down his cheeks.*

4. The coffee table bore its household harvest of books, periodicals, half-emptied coffee cups scummed over with cream, a dash of cigarette

7

ashes for good measure, and a heel of French bread. . . . An oval plat-
ter served as ashtray, heaped with a homey Vesuvius of cigarette butts,
ashes, bits of cellophane from discarded packs, a few martini-soaked
olive pits, and a final cigarette stub issuing a frail plume of smoke from
the top of the heap, signature of a dying volcano.[3]

5. He went out into the wind. Big holes were blown into the sky, the
moonlight blew about. Sometimes a high moon, liquid-brilliant, scudded
across a hollow space and took cover under electric, brown-iridescent
cloud-edges. Then there was a blot of cloud, and shadow. Then somewhere in the night a radiance again, like a vapour. And all the sky was
teeming and tearing along, a vast disorder of flying shapes and darkness
and ragged fumes of light and a great brown circling halo, then the terror
of a moon running liquid-brilliant into the open for a moment, hurting
the eyes before she plunged under cover of cloud again.[4]

1–8 Describing with Similes (*RHH*, 1d)

Working alone or with a group of classmates, use the following phrases to
create several fresh similes (avoid clichés: "flat as a pancake," "smooth as
silk"). List a number of possibilities for each phrase, even if some of them
sound forced or ungainly. Then use three of your best similes in descriptive
sentences. You might want to try for a humorous effect in one sentence.

Example: as flat as . . .

> the Kansas prairie, yesterday's
> Coke, a warm beer, a tomato
> under a truck tire, a soprano
> with a head cold

Descriptive Sentence:

> David was always the class clown,
> but his pranks were usually as
> flat as yesterday's Coke.

8

1. as red (or green, blue, yellow, etc.) as . . .

_____

_____

_____

_____

2. as messy as . . .

_____

_____

_____

_____

3. as confusing as . . .

_____

_____

_____

4. as smooth as . . .

_____

_____

_____

_____

5. as wrinkled as . . .

_____

_____

_____

_____

DESCRIPTIVE SENTENCES:

1. _____

_____

2. _____

_____

_____

_____

3. _____

_____

_____

_____

1–9 Changing Literal Language to Figurative Language (*RHH,* 1d)

In each of the following sentences, the italicized word is used in its literal sense. Write a descriptive sentence in which you use the same word figuratively.

Example: The children *played* in the yard for over an hour.

The day was nearly gone, but the sunlight played on the face of the cliff for a few more minutes before slipping away.

1. Andrew and Sarah *danced* gracefully across the floor.

_____

_____

2. Max *swam* twenty laps at the natatorium.

_____

_____

_____

3. Open your *mouth* and take a bite.

_____

_____

_____

4. *Eat* less and live longer.

_____

_____

_____

5. The flowers *wilted* in the afternoon sun.

_____

_____

_____

1–10 Recognizing Methods for Ordering a Description (*RHH*, 1e)

In the space provided, briefly explain the method used to organize each of the following descriptive passages. Be prepared to suggest at least one other way the author might have arranged the description. How would the alternative arrangement have changed the effect of the passage?

Example: Route 301, an inland route—to be taken in preference to the coast road, with its lines of trucks from the phosphate plants—passes through a lot of swampland, some scraggly pinewoods, and acre upon acre of strawberry beds covered with sheets of black plastic. There are fields where hairy, tough-looking cattle snatch at the grass between the palmettos. There are aluminum warehouses, cinder-block stores, and trailer homes in patches of dirt with laundry sailing out behind. There are Pentecostal churches and run-down cafes and bars with rows of pickup trucks parked out front.[5]

The passage describes sights that appear from a car traveling along Route 301. Natural landscapes are mentioned first (swampland, pinewoods); the sights become increasingly less rural as the paragraph progresses.

1. We heard a dull thumping on the side of the boat. When we looked over the side, the swimmer's head splashed to the surface, the water glistening on his smooth head and hanging in droplets from his whiskers. He tossed his head from side to side, opened his eyes, and looked at us curiously. Then suddenly the seal flipped backwards and glided out of sight, his tail slapping the surface as he disappeared.*

---

2. His voice was quiet, his movements slow and cautious. He stood in front of the desk, not behind the podium, dressed neatly in a pair of blue slacks, a slightly rumpled white shirt, and a gray knit tie. His shoes, newly polished, looked old, the heels worn smooth and the toes heavily creased. He was tall, but he slumped slightly, giving him a look of someone older that he probably was. His hair lay in thin wisps across the top of his head. What brought everything together was his beard: large, unruly, and flaming red. It took possession of the face, animating his whole figure and transfixing the class as he started his lecture.*

---

3. Travelers of back roads in southern New Mexico, southeastern Arizona, or northern Chihuahua and Sonora in Mexico may notice the broad, low

earthen mounds scattered over the desert flatlands. Anyone who stops to examine them will find that each mound has numerous holes that seem to be the entrances to tunnels or animal burrows. However, a daytime visitor who hopes for the animal occupants to emerge will inevitably be disappointed; they only come out after dark. On moonlit nights one can see them—creatures, a little bigger than hamsters, that hop on two legs like kangaroos and have long white-tipped tails. These last two features inspired their name—banner-tailed kangaroo rats.[6]

_____

_____

_____

_____

4. We left Martindale in a dense fog. The highway ahead looked like a dark tunnel illuminated by the car's headlights. By the time we got to Prairie Lea, we could see the gray shadows of trees along the highway looming dimly in the mist. The sun gradually burned its way into the fog, suffusing it with light, making the big oaks along the road stand out darkly in the white glow. Then suddenly the car broke out of the fog, and the trees emerged clear and green. For a few minutes more, scattered wisps of fog flew past the windows, but soon the day was clear and fresh, the sunlight glittering on the hood of the car.*

_____

_____

_____

_____

5. A fat brown goose lay at one end of the table and at the other end, on a bed of creased paper strewn with sprigs of parsley, lay a great ham, stripped of its outer skin and peppered over with crust crumbs, a neat paper frill round its shin and beside this was a round of spiced beef. Between these rival ends ran parallel lines of side-dishes: two little ministers of jelly, red and yellow, a shallow dish full of blocks of blancmange and red jam, a large green leaf-shaped dish with a stalk-shaped handle, on which lay bunches of purple raisins and peeled almonds, a companion dish on which lay a solid rectangle of Smyrna figs, a dish of custard topped with grated nutmeg, a small bowl of chocolates and

sweets wrapped in gold and silver papers and a glass vase in which stood some tall celery stalks. In the centre of the table there stood, as sentries to a fruit stand which upheld a pyramid of oranges and American apples, two squat old-fashioned decanters of cut glass, one containing port and the other dark sherry.[7]

_____

_____

_____

_____

1–11 Organizing a Brief Description (*RHH,* 1e)

Write a descriptive paragraph using one of the following topics. Use your own paper.

1. Study the organization of the second passage in Exercise 1–10. Use the same method to describe a person you know, beginning with secondary details and leading up to a dominant physical feature.
2. Study the organization of the fourth passage in Exercise 1–10. Then write a similar description, carefully evoking a change in the weather as you might observe it while traveling in a car.
3. Study the organization of the fifth passage in Exercise 1–10. Then use a similar organization to describe a table at a bake sale, a family dinner, a picnic, or a party.

1–12 Review Exercise: Identifying the Elements of an Effective Description (*RHH,* 1a–1e)

Working alone or with a group of classmates, study the following descriptive passages. For each passage, do the following:

1. Locate examples of concrete, specific language used to make the description vivid.
2. Identify the author's descriptive point of view—the physical perspective from which the scene is viewed.
3. Identify the author's attitude toward the subject matter and explain how that attitude is revealed.
4. Identify any figurative language used to sharpen the description.
5. Identify the method of organization used in the description.

14

1. [This passage, from an essay by George Orwell, begins just after the writer fires his rifle at an elephant that had earlier destroyed some property and killed a man.]

    In that instant, in too short a time, one would have thought, even for the bullet to get there, a mysterious, terrible change had come over the elephant. He neither stirred nor fell, but every line of his body had altered. He looked suddenly stricken, shrunken, immensely old, as though the frightful impact of the bullet had paralysed him without knocking him down. At last, after what seemed a long time—it might have been five seconds, I dare say—he sagged flabbily to his knees. His mouth slobbered. An enormous senility seemed to have settled upon him. One could have imagined him thousands of years old. I fired again into the same spot. At the second shot he did not collapse but climbed with desperate slowness to his feet and stood weakly upright, with legs sagging and head drooping. I fired a third time. That was the shot that did for him. You could see the agony of it jolt his whole body and knock the last remnant of strength from his legs. But in falling he seemed for a moment to rise, for as his hind legs collapsed beneath him he seemed to tower upward like a huge rock toppling, his trunk reaching skywards like a tree. He trumpeted, for the first and only time. And then down he came, his belly towards me, with a crash that seemed to shake the ground even where I lay.[8]

2. [This passage, from a short story by Eudora Welty, describes an old woman who walks several miles to buy medicine for her ailing grandson.]

    Far out in the country there was an old Negro woman with her head tied in a red rag, coming along a path through the pinewoods. Her name was Phoenix Jackson. She was very old and small and she walked slowly in the dark pine shadows, moving a little from side to side in her steps, with the balanced heaviness and lightness of a pendulum in a grandfather clock. She carried a thin, small cane made from an umbrella, and with this she kept tapping the frozen earth in front of her. This made a grave and persistent noise in the still air that seemed meditative, like the chirping of a solitary little bird.
    She wore a dark striped dress reaching down to her shoetops, and an equally long apron of bleached sugar sacks, with a full pocket: all neat and tidy, but every time she took a step she might have fallen over her shoelaces, which dragged from her unlaced shoes. She looked

straight ahead. Her eyes were blue with age. Her skin had a pattern all its own of numberless branching wrinkles and as though a whole little tree stood in the middle of her forehead, but a golden color ran underneath, and the two knobs of her cheeks were illumined by a yellow burning under the dark. Under the red rag her hair came down on her neck in the frailest of ringlets, still black, and with an odor like copper.[9]

NARRATION

1–13 Changing a Narrative from Past to Present Tense (*RHH*, 1g)

The following paragraph is the opening of "Father's Day," a narrative essay written for a freshman composition course. The student used past tense. In the space above the lines, change the verbs to present tense. Be prepared to discuss how the change in tense affects the narrative. The first verb is done for you as an example.

1   We w*are*̶e̶ sitting around the house on Saturday morning as we gen-

erally do, drinking coffee and watching cartoons. My wife Nancy,

who was nine and a half months pregnant, started having contrac-

tions. This didn't surprise or worry me, for she had been having

5   them off and on for the past couple of days. We waited half an hour

and then decided to time the contractions. They were coming about

ten minutes apart. I tried to help Nancy with her breathing, using the

Lamaze techniques we practiced in our childbirth classes. An hour

later, the contractions stopped, but they soon started again, and after

10   another hour of non-stop, closely spaced contractions, Nancy finally

agreed that it was time to go to the hospital. I called the doctor. As

my wife packed her bag, I walked around in circles smoking a cig-

arette, not knowing what else to do with myself.*

1-14 Using Past and Present Tense in a Narrative (*RHH*, 1g)

Recall a fairy tale or fable you heard as a child. Write one version of the story using past tense. Then write a second version using present tense. Use your own paper. Bring the two versions to class, and be prepared to discuss the following:

1. How does the change in verb tense affect the story?
2. Which tense seems more appropriate for a fairy tale or fable? Why?
3. If you were to tell your story to a group of children, would you use past tense or present tense? Why?

Note: If you have trouble recalling an appropriate story for this exercise, try brainstorming with a group of classmates.

1-15 Converting a Narrative from Direct to Indirect Discourse (*RHH*, 1h)

The following brief narrative uses direct discourse to report an incident in a straightforward fashion. Rewrite the passage, relying primarily on indirect discourse (dialogue) to enliven the incident and to give it greater immediacy. Use your own paper.

> The interviewer asked Winston about the *D* on his transcript, the one in algebra. Feeling suddenly defensive, Winston explained that he was a freshman at the time, was unprepared for the course, and had spent too much of his time pledging a fraternity. The interviewer made a sound suggesting that he wasn't very impressed by the explanation. There was a long pause which Winston interrupted by saying that his subsequent math grades, while not outstanding, were somewhat higher. The interviewer looked tired, shrugged his shoulders, and suddenly asked Winston why he wanted to work for the IRS.

1-16 Using Anticipatory Narration (*RHH*, 1i)

Reread the two versions of a fairy tale or fable that you wrote for Exercise 1-14. Rewrite the story using anticipatory narration. Use your own paper. Start with a dramatic scene from the end of the story (when the frog turns into a prince or the tortoise crosses the finish line ahead of the hare). Then move back to the beginning, and narrate the events leading up to the passage with which you opened the story. Bring your narrative to class, and be prepared to discuss the following questions:

1. How does the use of anticipatory narration affect the story?
2. What advantages does the story teller gain by using anticipatory narration? What are the drawbacks of the method?
3. If you were to tell your story to a group of young children, would you use anticipatory narration? Why?

1–17 Using Narrative to Make an Implied Point (*RHH*, 1j)

We frequently rely on familiar sayings—proverbs, maxims, truisms—to explain human behavior or to comment on the world around us. Write a narrative in which you illustrate the truth of one of the following sayings. Use your own paper. The point of your narrative should be implied. Don't state the conclusion openly; let the story lead the reader to see the point. Feel free to use another saying if the following list doesn't contain one that appeals to you.

SAYINGS

All that glitters is not gold.

Everyone has his or her price.

Don't count your chickens before they're hatched.

Don't judge a book by its cover.

Don't cry over spilled milk.

Don't cut off your nose to spite your face.

He who laughs last, laughs best.

A bird in the hand is worth two in the bush.

The grass is always greener on the other side of the fence.

Haste makes waste.—*Benjamin Franklin*

He that lies down with dogs, shall rise up with fleas.—*Benjamin Franklin*

When the well's dry, we know the worth of water.—*Benjamin Franklin*

1–18 Review Exercises: Analyzing a Narrative Essay (*RHH*, 1f–j)

Working alone or with a group of classmates, study the student narrative essay printed below. Then answer the following questions. Use your own paper.

1. Does the writer bring the qualities of an effective description to bear in writing the narrative? Identify specific passages that make use of descriptive language.

2. The writer uses present tense. Is the choice a wise one? How would the narrative differ if she had used present tense?

3. How effective is the opening of the narrative? What effect does the writer gain by gradually letting us know what she does for a living rather than revealing the information at the beginning?

4. How could the writer have used anticipatory narration? Suggest a specific way in which she might have opened the story.

5. What unifies the narrative, gives it purpose? Does it have an implied point? Does it create a dominant mood? Explain.

6. In an early draft of the narrative, the student included the following paragraph at the point noted in the text:

> I come to the conclusion that I should do laundry, but it has started raining harder, and I realize that I will never be able to get my truck off the lot in all this mud. It always surprises me that the show can still find an empty field for the tent in this part of the country. When we drove in this morning the highway seemed to wind through a continuous stream of concrete buildings, making it difficult to tell one town from the next—a real concrete jungle. And yet the agent found another space for our little mobile village. I will be glad to get back to the part of the country where there are trees and mountains and clear running streams. But money dictates, and the money is here. The rain dripping off the top of the tent onto my head brings me back to reality and I get up and clear my plate.*

Was the writer wise to delete this paragraph in the final version of the essay? What is gained by the deletion? What is lost?

Behind the Scenes

As I reach for the alarm clock, I think of two things: I'm glad I remembered to wind it last night, and I wish I could get another three hours sleep. But it's already 5:20, so I crawl out of bed and start getting ready to make the move.

My trailer is well organized, so only a few items need to be set down on the floor: the television, a handful of pictures, and the plants. The plants are the most difficult thing to relocate for each move, and I often think of getting rid of them. But they add such a homey touch that I usually only grumble about them at 5:30 in the morning.

The drive today is seventy-five miles, a fairly typical move for the circus. But it will be difficult because the show is moving from Long Island to a small town on the other side of New York City. There was talk of making the move last night to avoid all the traffic, but some of the trucks didn't have working lights and might have been ticketed.

As I climb into my truck with a thermos of coffee, I see that nearly all the other vehicles are already gone; most of the show trucks left thirty minutes ago, their drivers refreshed with a strong cup of coffee and a couple of sweet rolls. Breakfast isn't served until we make it to the next lot, a rather obvious carrot tactic.

As I drive along the highway, I keep an eye out for the small red and white paper arrows that tell me where to turn or where the lot is going to be. The show was lucky today; oftentimes the highway patrol removes the arrows from the telephone poles or highway markers. We are given route slips to compensate for that eventuality, and today the slip proves very helpful even though most of the arrows are still up. All the traffic makes me nervous, and the exit for the Verrazano Bridge nearly slips by me. It has started to rain.

Finally, the seventy-five miles are behind me and my thermos is empty. I have arrived at the circus lot. The tent is already stretched out, and the elephant has started pulling up the side poles. I drive my truck and trailer into the backyard where the performers are supposed to park. I try to find a fairly level spot for my home on wheels and then make my way over to the cookhouse.

The flag is still up over the tent that covers the tables where breakfast is being served. I wait in line behind several other performers who are trying to stay dry by huddling under the wing of the cook truck. It is under this wing and through the window it protects that I occasionally see a hand passing out a plate of grits, eggs, toast, and bacon. The line moves along rather quickly considering that Doris the cook really does prepare the eggs the way we want them. As I sit alone in the tent eating my breakfast, I review the list of things that need my attention today. One thing about life in a circus, you quickly learn to do two things at once; wasting time is a major offense. If you are not doing two things, you are at least thinking about doing something else.

The rain this morning is going to slow everything down. I can usually set up my equipment by ten-thirty. Today I probably won't get up the tight wire and trapeze until noon.

[Draft paragraph deleted at this point. See Item 6, page 19.]

After breakfast I walk back to the trailer and start performing some of the rituals of the day. I put the plants and TV back in place and survey the trailer to see if there is any damage from the drive. Fortunately everything has stayed in place.

Because it is raining, I get out costumes that won't be ruined by the weather; feathers are out of the question. It begins to cross my mind that much of the rest of the world is cozy and dry on this rainy gray Tuesday. I start thinking about a house on a foundation instead of a house on wheels. I think of people working in a dry safe building instead of working in a leaky dangerous tent. I think about the security that a "real" job provides, and then I remember the applause. I put on my galoshes and go out to set up my props.

I takes me about an hour and a half to put my rigging together. The prop boss helps me drive the long iron stakes into the ground. Today the ground is soft and the work is easier; sometimes it feels as if I have to pound the stakes through concrete. Some of the other performers pay the prop hands to put up their rigging, especially on days like today. But my dad always said that one mistake in setting up the equipment could cost me my life, and that isn't something to put in someone else's hands.

As I finish the last of the dirty work I think about the fact that the audience sees me perform for ten minutes on the trapeze and for seven minutes on the tight wire. I wonder if they ever consider all the behind-the-scenes work that goes into that seventeen-minute performance. I realize that they probably don't.*

2

Strategies of Analysis and Argument

2–1 Identifying Strategies of Analysis: Definition (*RHH*, 2a)

Study the use of definition in the following passages. Then answer the questions that follow. Be prepared to discuss your answers in class.

1.   There are many theories, all unproved, as to how language began. Most picturesque among them is the "bow-wow" hypothesis, to the effect that men began to speak by imitating the natural sounds they heard, or thought they heard, around them.

      The barking of a dog would strike the ear of the leader of a small band of primitive humans. It would sound to him like "bow-wow," and as he tried to imitate it, he would convey to the others, by pointing to the dog and repeating "bow-wow," that the creatures that made that particular sound should henceforth be referred to as "bow-wow."

      Too simple? Yet consider how often children spontaneously fasten upon some utterance produced by one of their number, and use it to designate him, pointing to him in derision as they do it.

The scientific name for this process is *onomatopoeia,* or "name-making." Less scientific but easier to pronounce and spell is "echoic word." You echo what you hear. If the fall of a big tree in the forest sounds to you like "crash," that is what you use to designate that type of sound. The noise produced by a bee may sound like "hum" or "buzz." Words like "click," "wham," "bang" all seem to be of echoic origin.[10]

NOTES FOR CLASS DISCUSSION

a. What is defined in the passage? _____
_____
_____

b. What method does the author use to construct the definition? _____
_____
_____
_____
_____
_____

c. The third paragraph is not part of the definition. What purpose does it serve?
_____
_____
_____
_____
_____
_____

2. The word *orange* evolved from Sanskrit. The Chinese word for orange, in ancient as well as modern Chinese, is *jyu,* but it did not migrate with the fruit. India was the first major stop in the westward travels of citrus, and the first mention of oranges in Sanskrit literature is found in a medical book called the *Charaka-Samhita,* which was compiled approximately two thousand years ago. The Hindus called an orange a *naranga,* the first syllable of which, according to Tolkowsky, was a prefix meaning fragrance. This became the Persian *naranj,* a word the Muslims carried through the Mediterranean. In Byzantium, an orange was a *nerantzion.* This, in Neo-Latin, became variously styled as *arangium, arantium,* and *aurantium*—eventually producing *naranja* in Spain, *laranja* in Portugal, *arancia* in Italy, and *orange* in France.[11]

NOTES FOR CLASS DISCUSSION

a. What method does the author use to define the word *orange?* _____

_____

_____

_____

b. What does the definition contribute to our understanding of oranges?

_____

_____

_____

_____

c. Would the definition be helpful to someone who had never seen an orange? Why?

_____

_____

_____

_____

3. My grandmother, my mother, and I are philatelists—just three of the many thousands of philatelists living in the United States. No, we don't belong to a secret cult, nor do we practice strange rituals. While the

word may sound strange, its meaning is quite simple. A philatelist is a stamp collector, one who loves postage stamps. Philatelists collect and study postage stamps, stamped envelopes, post marks, post cards, and all the paraphernalia connected with postal history. Most people know at least something about stamp collecting, if only from recent efforts by the U.S. Postal Service to promote the hobby. But philately today is far more than a hobby; it is a big business in which investors spend millions of dollars speculating in rare stamps.*

NOTES FOR CLASS DISCUSSION

a. This passage is the introduction to a student essay about stamp collecting as a business investment. What does the writer gain by using definition to begin her essay?

_____

_____

_____

_____

b. *Philatelist* and *philately* are specialized terms. Why do you think the writer decided to use them even though she wasn't writing for an audience of specialists?

_____

_____

_____

_____

_____

2–2 Developing Ideas: Definition (*RHH,* 2a)

Working alone or with a group of classmates, develop ideas for an extended definition. First, select a term complex enough to warrant an extended definition. Then brainstorm, listing ideas and examples that might be useful in writing the definition. Possible topics: freedom, patriotism, conservatism, parental love, sexism.

Example: Term _Charity_

Ideas and Examples *personal charity – kindness to others, volunteer work, Good Samaritan / organized charity – donating money, church and government help for the needy, benefit concerts for the hungry . . .*

Term _____

Ideas and Examples _____

_____

_____

_____

_____

_____

_____

_____

_____

_____

_____

2–3 Writing Practice: Using Definition (*RHH,* 2a)

Write a paragraph, a series of paragraphs, or a complete essay using definition as a strategy of analysis. Use your own paper. Try one of the following topics or use one of your own.

1. Write an extended definition of the term you worked with in Exercise 2–2. Construct your definition by developing several of the ideas and examples

25

recorded in the earlier exercise. Your notes may contain more material than you need, so take care to focus your topic before you begin to write.

2. Reread the definition paragraph about oranges in Exercise 2-1. Write a much different kind of paragraph, one aimed at defining the word *orange* for someone who has never seen, felt, or tasted an orange, or do the same thing for another fruit or vegetable.

3. Reread the paragraph about stamp collecting in Exercise 2-1. Then write a similar paragraph in which you introduce a hobby, trade, profession, or other activity by defining its technical name. Suggested topics: spelunker, numismatist, lapidarist, discographer, ichthyologist.

4. Slang terms are difficult to define because their meanings shift rapidly and depend heavily on the group of people using them. Define one of the following terms (or one of your own choice) for someone who has never heard it before: *turkey, dude, teenybopper, yuppie, burnout.* Use examples to make your definition sharp and vivid. If the term has different meanings in different contexts, acknowledge that fact in writing your definition.

2-4 Identifying Strategies of Analysis: Division (*RHH,* 2b)

Study the use of division in the following passages. Then answer the questions that follow. Be prepared to discuss your answers in class.

1. Sight can be defined in four basic ways. In its most fundamental form, it is the ability to detect the difference between light and darkness. For most simple life forms, from amoebas to earthworms, or for fishes that live in the depths of the ocean, this is about all their eyes can handle.

Far more important to the majority of the animal kindgom is the second visual skill—the ability to detect movement. This is most important to those animals, such as insects, that must move rapidly to catch food or to flee, and for animals that are often hunted, like mice and rabbits.

Most predatory animals such as hawks and lions rely more on a third skill—form vision—which is the ability to see and recognize the shape or nature of an object. In human terms we measure form vision by the ability to recognize letters on an eye chart. For animals, those forms may become a suitable mate, or a meal, or a predator.

The fourth dimension of sight is color vision, the ability to see specific wavelengths of visible light. Color vision is present in some insects, fishes and reptiles, and is possessed by most birds and reptiles.[12]

NOTES FOR CLASS DISCUSSION

a. The author identifies four types of sight. List them here.

_____

_____

_____

_____

b. How does the author organize the passage? What principle does he use
to arrange the four types of sight?

_____

_____

_____

_____

c. Besides division, what strategies of analysis are used in the passage?
Explain. _____

_____

_____

_____

2.   During the past month, the *Star* has published several columns and
letters addressing the widely publicized parking problem on campus.
The main issues are well known: campus construction projects have
gobbled up most of the prime parking spots near classroom buildings;
dorm residents are bringing cars to campus in increasing numbers each
year; and the overall campus population—students, faculty, and staff—
has grown faster than the number of available parking spaces.
        Most of the proposed solutions to the parking problem fall into two
broad categories: those that require more land and those that restrict access to prime parking spaces, usually by giving preferred status to
faculty, staff, and seniors. As for the first solution, land is in very short
supply on the central campus, and, as others have pointed out, using it
for parking seems unwise. The other solution, restricted access to parking, displeases the many students who will be denied space.

I believe that there is a third alternative, one that will save land and keep nearly everybody happy: a multi-level parking facility on the central campus.*

NOTES FOR CLASS DISCUSSION

a. The writer uses division as a strategy of analysis in both the first and second paragraphs. What purpose does the strategy serve in the first paragraph? _____

_____

_____

_____

In the second paragraph? _____

_____

_____

_____

b. Having used division to present two unworkable solutions to the parking problem, the writer offers his own solution. What objections might be raised to his idea?_____

_____

_____

_____

2–5 Developing Ideas: Division (*RHH,* 2b)

Develop several ways of dividing the members of your composition class (or another group of people) into categories. The possibilities are nearly endless, so use your imagination. First write the basis for making a division (hair color); then list the various categories you find in the group (blond, black, red, etc.). Other possibilities: ethnic origin, age, state where born, reason for attending college.

Example: Basis for Division   *place of residence*

Categories _parents' home - 7 /_
dorm - 12 / apartment - 3 /
own home - 1

Basis for Division _____

Categories _____
_____
_____
_____

Basis for Division _____

Categories _____
_____
_____
_____

Basis for Division _____

Categories _____
_____
_____
_____

Basis for Division _____

Categories _____
_____
_____
_____

Basis for Division _____

Categories _____

_____

_____

2–6   Writing Practice: Division (*RHH,* 2b)

Write a paragraph, a series of paragraphs, or a complete essay using division as a strategy of analysis. Try one of the following topics or use one of your own.

1. Use the notes you recorded in Exercise 2–5 to write several paragraphs describing the group you analyzed. Try to make several generalizations about the group, basing your conclusions on the categories you devised. (Obviously, information such as "reason for attending college" will be more useful than "hair color.")
2. Reread the passage about eyesight in Exercise 2–4. Write a similar passage, dividing one of the other senses into three or four categories. Rather than using technical information, rely on your own experience to suggest various ways in which we use our senses. Give examples to illustrate each category.
3. Write a paragraph or two categorizing the types of bumper stickers you observe during a week.
4. Take an inventory of everything in and on top of your desk. Divide the items into several categories (you may have to include a "miscellaneous" category). Write a few paragraphs explaining what you learned from this exercise in division. You may want to do the same exercise with the contents of your purse, wallet, closet, refrigerator, or glove compartment.

2–7   Identifying Strategies of Analysis: Illustration (*RHH,* 2c)

Study the use of illustration in the following passages. Then answer the questions that follow. Be prepared to discuss your answers in class.

1. West Germany is experiencing an Americanization of its language.
    Most of the English-language expressions that have crept into German conversation in recent times have come from science, the drug

scene, and popular culture. But even ordinary West German citizens find that American terms are now part of their everyday lives.

For example, Germans often wear *jeans, T-shirts, sweat shirts,* and *pullovers.* They talk about the *job* and the *boss,* and they eat *fast food.*

Those who are *champions* at international travel belong to the *jet set* and are called *globis.* They know all about *boarding cards, check-ins, stand-bys, no-shows,* and *charters.* When their plans change, they don't hesitate to *cancel* their *first-class* and *economy* reservations.

Everyone, of course, knows about *love* and *sex.* In many instances, in fact, *sex* is better than *Geschlechtsverkehr,* which tends to be a vulgar way of saying the same thing.

Germany's younger generation, especially the *teen-agers* and *teenies,* are particularly fond of American terms, which they often combine with German words. They talk about *Powerstimmung* (a great mood) and *irres feeling* (a great feeling), which can make them *ganz high,* if not also *ausgeplippt.*[13]

NOTES FOR CLASS DISCUSSION

a. What point is the writer illustrating?

_____

_____

_____

b. What is the function of the second paragraph?

_____

_____

_____

c. For the third through sixth paragraphs, indicate the category of words used to illustrate the writer's point.

Paragraph 3 _____

Paragraph 4 _____

Paragraph 5 _____

Paragraph 6 _____

2.   In the first act of Henrik Ibsen's play, *A Doll's House,* Nora Helmer adopts a different personality for each character she talks with. To her husband, Torvald, Nora is a "songbird." She constantly whirls around him and does everything possible to win his praise, acting coy, flirtatious, and helpless. When she first talks with Mrs. Linde, a childhood friend, Nora acts like a young high school girl. She brags about her husband's promotion at work much like a cheerleader might brag about her boyfriend's being named captain of the football team. But when it comes to conversing with Mr. Krogstad, Torvald's employee, Nora is no longer a "songbird" or a cheerleader; she now becomes a serious, forceful woman.

   Why can't Nora be this same serious woman when she talks with her husband?*

NOTES FOR CLASS DISCUSSION

a.   This passage is the introduction to a student essay analyzing a character in a play. What does the writer gain by using illustration to begin her essay?

_____

_____

_____

_____

b.   What effect does the writer achieve by including only one sentence in her second paragraph?

_____

_____

_____

_____

2–8 Developing Ideas: Illustration (*RHH,* 2c)

Working alone or with a group of classmates, formulate several general statements. Then make a list of illustrations that might be developed to support each one. Possible topics: the campus library, group behavior, students' attitudes toward poetry (or anything else), popular rock lyrics, country music.

Example: General Statement _A word processor greatly eases the problems of writing a research paper._

Illustrations _research notes stored on disk, questions easily inserted into paper without recopying, paragraphs and longer passages shifted around with little retyping, reference list alphabetized and edited quickly..._

General Statement _____

_____

Illustrations _____

_____

_____

_____

_____

_____

_____

General Statement _____

_____

Illustrations _____

_____

_____

_____

_____

_____

General Statement _____

_____

Illustrations _____

_____

_____

_____

_____

_____

2–9 Writing Practice: Illustration (*RHH*, 2c)

Write a paragraph, a series of paragraphs, or a complete essay using illustration as a strategy of analysis. Try one of the following topics or use one of your own. Use your own paper.

1. Write a paragraph or series of paragraphs beginning with one of the general statements you formulated in Exercise 2–8. Select a few of the best illustrations you listed; then develop them to support your point.
2. Reread the passage in Exercise 2–7 about the "Americanization" of the German language. Then write a similar passage beginning with the following general statement: Americans use slang in nearly every aspect of their everyday lives. Illustrate the statement with several brief paragraphs, each one giving examples from a particular aspect of daily life. Example: words referring to entertainment—TV, show biz, sitcom, flicks.
3. Reread the passage in Exercise 2–7 about Ibsen's *A Doll's House*. Then write a similar passage illustrating a general statement about a character in another story, novel, play, or movie.

4. Write a paragraph or series of paragraphs illustrating one of the following general statements:

Recent movies support the notion that Americans are fascinated by violence.

People with good ideas are often ignored.

Several of the buildings on campus illustrate the very best (or worst) in contemporay architecture.

Procrastination is one of the worst vices of college students.

2–10 Identifying Strategies of Analysis: Cause and Effect (*RHH,* 2d)

Study the cause-effect relationships in the following passages. Then answer the questions that follow. Be prepared to discuss your answers in class.

1. As the world went into war [World War II] men and women went into uniform. Occasions for dressing up understandably dwindled, and most people made do with wearing their old clothes or with having them refurbished. All new clothing manufacture was governed by the War Production Board, and double-breasted and other fabric-thirsty styles for men were prohibited. Suits no longer came automatically with vests, and thereafter vests would be an "extra" in a man's wardrobe. Also regulated were cuffs, pocket flaps, and vents. With clothing coupons in short supply, dinner clothes were not much of a priority.

Women's clothes suffered, perhaps more, in the process. Skirts had to be short, just below the knee, and fairly skimpy, in order to meet with the yardage restrictions. Jackets were long and straight and broad at the shoulders. Dresses were usually of imitation silk. In occupied Paris, many of the couture houses closed down completely, and it was thus that American designers had their first chance in the spotlight. Already accustomed to working with the restrictions of mass-production, designers such as Claire McCardell, Norell, Adrian, and Mainbocher proved adept at making wearable clothes with whatever was at hand. Among the materials rationed were metal, wood, leather, silk, and nylon, and women took to wearing cork-platformed shoes, painting their legs suntan in lieu of wearing stockings, and concocting hats out of "found objects."[14]

35

NOTES FOR CLASS DISCUSSION

a. World War II is the primary "cause" of the changes described in the passage. Make a list summarizing the "effects" of the war on clothing styles.

_____

_____

_____

_____

_____

_____

_____

_____

b. Some of the effects described in the passage are very specific (dresses made of imitation silk). What larger economic "effects" of the War are stated or implied in the passage?

_____

_____

_____

_____

_____

c. What other strategy of analysis might the writer have used to describe changes in fashion during the war years? Explain.

_____

_____

_____

2. We think of males as large and powerful, females as smaller and weaker, but the opposite pattern prevails throughout nature—males are generally

smaller than females, and for good reason, humans and most other mammals notwithstanding. Sperm is small and cheap, easily manufactured in large quantities by little creatures. A sperm cell is little more than a nucleus of naked DNA with a delivery system. Eggs, on the other hand, must be larger, for they provide the cytoplasm (all the rest of the cell) with mitochondria (or energy factories), chloroplasts (for photosynthesizers), and all other parts that a zygote needs to begin the process of embryonic growth. In addition, eggs generally supply the initial nutriment, or food for the developing embryo. Finally, females usually perform the tasks of primary care, either retaining the eggs within their bodies for a time or guarding them after they are laid. For all these reasons, females are larger than males in most species of animals.[15]

NOTES FOR CLASS DISCUSSION

a. What "effect" does the author explain in the passage?

_____

_____

_____

b. What are the "causes" of this "effect"?

_____

_____

_____

_____

_____

c. Describe the organization of the paragraph. Where does the author state the effect? Where the causes?

_____

_____

_____

_____

d. What strategies besides cause-effect analysis are used in the passage?

_____

_____

_____

_____

_____

_____

_____

2–11 Examining Cause and Effect as a Strategy for Essay Development (*RHH*, 2d)

Cause-effect analysis is often used as the controlling strategy for an entire piece of writing. In the following essay, for example, the strategy serves as a primary means of development and as an organizational device. Study the essay carefully. Then construct an outline showing the sequence of cause-effect relationships it develops. Use your own paper, and be prepared to discuss your findings in class.

Death from the Sky
Sam Iker

The ultimate environmental calamity which might result from nuclear war would be the destruction of the fragile stratospheric layer of ozone which shields the planet from the deadly effects of ultraviolet radiation.

A nuclear detonation of sufficient size (more than one megaton) can inject large amounts of oxides of nitrogen into the stratosphere. Through a complex set of chemical reactions, this can result in the destruction of ozone. Atmospheric scientists, using the most sophisticated computer models, calculate that a full-scale nuclear exchange would wipe out around 50 percent of the ozone layer. This could double or triple the intensity of the most hazardous portion of the ultraviolet spectrum reaching the Earth. Some analysts believe that the trend toward smaller, more precisely guided weapons lessens this threat. But others feel that the heavier yield warheads remaining in the Soviet arsenal make the danger very real.

If the pessimists are right, the potential impacts would be cataclysmic. Scientists agree that the existence of the ozone layer enabled life to develop on the planet. Without its shielding effect (even for the two or three years it would take for the layer to partially regenerate), most living organisms would be threatened.

Human beings are especially vulnerable. Even at present levels, ultraviolet radiation causes great numbers of cases of skin cancer among those exposed excessively to the sun. If the radiation were increased by 200 or 300 percent, people couldn't remain outdoors for more than a few minutes at a time without risking life-threatening sunburn (unless they were completely protected).

Most animals and birds would be shielded by their feathers or fur. But their eyes would be vulnerable to the intense ultraviolet rays. According to University of Houston professor Donald Pitts, an authority on such effects, the exposures would cause "permanent damage to the cornea." Says Pitts, "Animals such as cattle, sheep, hogs, deer and so on would be rendered blind." Even birds and insects would lose their sight. The ecological implications are staggering.

Aquatic life would be equally vulnerable. Eggs, larvae and juveniles, which generally are found near the water's surface, have no way of detecting intensified ultraviolet rays (nor do they have effective natural defenses). Increased radiation, researchers find, is often lethal to such organisms. Many species of phytoplankton are also killed by powerful ultraviolet light. With mass die-offs of phytoplankton and zooplankton, says NOAA marine biologist David Damkaer, "the food chain is derailed. It's a domino effect."

Some crops are fairly resistant to ultraviolet radiation. But others, such as corn, sugar beets, tomatoes, beans and peas are highly sensitive. The rays affect the DNA of such plants and also retard the photosynthesis process. Most research (which is ongoing) has been done on commercial crops. Scientists still lack a detailed understanding of what the intensified radiation would do to other vegetation.

Even the global climate could be temporarily disrupted by the depletion of the ozone layer. More sunlight would reach the Earth and thus raise world temperatures. At the same time, however, less heat would be radiated back to the Earth by the thinned-out ozone layer. Given the immense complexities involved, the climatic impacts are uncertain. But even relatively minor changes in world weather patterns could disrupt or even devastate global ecosystems.[16]

2–12   Developing Ideas: Cause and Effect (*RHH*, 2d)

A. Working alone or with a group of classmates, explore the causes of a particular effect. First, name an effect—an event, a fact, a natural phenomenon—that can be linked to a number of possible causes. Then use brainstorming to list as many of those causes as you can. After completing the list, discuss which causes are most likely to be minor and which most significant.

Example: Effect   *the popularity of blue jeans*

Causes _durable, easy to care_
for, comfortable, adaptable
for formal or casual wear,
subtle pressure to conform
(everyone wears them),
sizes for everyone . . .

Effect _____

Causes _____

_____

_____

_____

_____

_____

_____

_____

_____

_____

B. Now reverse the procedure you used in Part A. Name a cause—an event, a fact, a natural phenomenon—that is likely to have a variety of effects or consequences. You may name an actual cause or imagine one (What if x happened?). Then use brainstorming to develop a list of as many possible effects as you can.

Example: Cause _exposure to the sun_

Effects _source of vitamin D,_
sunburn, suntan, dry skin,
itching, long-term risk of
skin cancer . . .

Cause _____

Effects _____

_____

_____

_____

_____

_____

_____

_____

_____

2-13 Writing Practice: Cause and Effect (*RHH,* 2d)

Write a paragraph, a series of paragraphs, or a complete essay using cause and effect analysis as a strategy of development. Try one of the following topics or use one of your own. Use you own paper.

1. Write a paragraph or series of paragraphs explaining one of the cause-effect relationships you explored in Exercise 2-14. Focus your attention on developing major causes or effects, relegating minor ones to secondary status or omitting them entirely.
2. Reread the passage on clothing styles in Exercise 2-10. Then write a similar passage showing how a particular political or social event (cause) changed clothing styles (effect). Possible causes: the women's movement, the sexual revolution, the new conservatism of the 1980s, the war in Vietnam.
3. Reread the passage on male/female size difference in Exercise 2-10, noting how the author carefully explains the causes of the difference. Then use an encyclopedia or other reference work to look up a natural phenomenon that arouses your curiosity. Read the source and write a paragraph or series of paragraphs explaining the cause(s) of the phenomenon you studied. Possible topics: cause of a certain type of weather, of a rainbow, of whales stranding themselves on beaches, of dinosaurs becoming extinct, of a firefly's glow.

4. Write a paragraph, series of paragraphs, or an entire essay explaining one of the following:

Effects of aging as you observe them in yourself or in someone you know

Effects of falling in love (feel free to treat this topic seriously or humorously)

Causes for the popularity of a particular singer, actor, or politician

Causes for your success at accomplishing something difficult (giving up cigarettes, earning a good grade in your chemistry course, learning to speak French)

2–14 Identifying Strategies of Development: Comparison and Contrast (*RHH*, 2e)

Study the use of comparison and contrast in the following passages. Then answer the questions that follow. Be prepared to discuss your answers in class.

1.   It takes a conscious effort to realize how constricted the space is on a basketball court. Place a regulation court (ninety-four by fifty feet) on a football field, and it will reach from the back of the end zone to the twenty-one-yard line; its width will cover less than a third of the field. On a baseball diamond, a basketball court will reach from home plate to just beyond first base. Compared to its principal indoor rival, ice hockey, basketball covers about one-fourth the playing area. And during the normal flow of the game, most of the action takes place on about the third of the court nearest the basket. It is in this dollhouse space that ten men, each of them half a foot taller than the average man, come together to battle each other.[17]

NOTES FOR CLASS DISCUSSION

a. What is the author comparing? _____

_____

_____

b. What is the purpose of the comparison? In other words, what point does the author make?

_____

_____

_____

_____

c. How is the paragraph organized? Consider especially the function of the first and last sentences.

_____

_____

_____

_____

_____

2.   In the early history of the American family farm, the cow was the foundation animal for the homestead. It supplied both meat and milk. Today, however, the goat is a practical alternative for a homesteader with an acre or two of land. It offers all the advantages of the dairy cow with none of the drawbacks.

The greatest advantage of the goat is its small size. A cow pastured on an acre or two of grazing land needs supplemental food. A pair of goats, however, can manage nicely on as little as an acre. Any land not needed for grazing can be used for other homesteading purposes. And the meat and milk produced by a pair of goats should be adequate for most families. The goat's small size also means less space for shelter in the winter months.

Manure is a welcome byproduct in any homesteading operation (it makes excellent fertilizer), but too much of it creates problems with disposal. Goats produce less manure than cows do, both because of their size and because they process their food more completely. Furthermore, the form of goat manure—relatively dry "berries"—makes it easier to handle than cow manure, and these "berries" seldom leave the disagreeable odor that cow manure does. The advantages for the homesteader are greater ease of handling and a manure supply that doesn't create an unusable excess each year.

A city person might not consider the third advantage of goats: companionship. They are similar to dogs in their responsiveness and attachment to a family. The yearly crop of kids provides a marvelous diversion, especially for children. Cows, on the other hand, are cows, not pets.*

NOTES FOR CLASS DISCUSSION

a. What is the author comparing?

_____

_____

_____

b. What is the purpose of the comparison? In other words what point does the author make?

_____

_____

_____

_____

c. How is the passage organized? List the topics developed in the second, third, and fourth paragraphs.

_____

_____

_____

3.   **Teacher's Tests**
                        Pierre Szamek

Doris Green, a seventh-grade teacher in Akron, Ohio, is twenty-nine. She has taught for six years. She is proud of her work and serves it conscientiously. "I'm a good teacher, I think," she says. "Anyway, I like the kids, and that's what it's all about, isn't it?"

In her home state of New Jersey, Doris Green was moved casually through the full program of state teacher-training requirements at Newark State College (now Kean College). Taking the complete battery of prescribed courses, she received all of the required grades: an A in Educational Psychology, course number 3501 ("This course considers cognition, motivation, tests and measurements. . . ."); an A in Educational Psychology, 4501 ("Group Dynamics . . . , Group Function, Group Structure, Communication, Means of Observing, Group Information. . . ."); an A in Creative Techniques; an A in Health Education, 4333 ("Alcohol and Narcotics Education"); and wound up with a B plus in Language Arts. With these suitably accomplished, she topped the list with eight of the ten courses offered in Reading Education.

Among these, the course she enjoyed most was Reading Education 4103. "We worked on the relation of intonation to meaning," she explains, "which is something I had never thought of before. I guess this is what makes education so exciting; it opens up so many new worlds."

Doris Green graduated from her teacher-training program with a near A average. After a one-semester practice-teaching period, she received her $13,000-a-year position within three months of graduation.

Armand Forestier, the thirty-three-year-old schoolmaster of a three-room school in Arcy-sur-Aube, a French town ninety miles west of Paris, followed a somewhat different road.

After graduating from the lycée, M. Forestier entered university, immersing himself in a six-year program of French history, French literature, and Romance philology, two years of philosophy, and a well-balanced science program combining six years of physics and chemistry.

Upon satisfactory qualification in these subjects, he was given the final written and oral tests that, when sustained, allowed him to apply for a teaching position at the primary level. So difficult is this examination that in a recent test given to 4,781 candidates, only 681 passed. Of those who failed, most were stopped by the meticulous demands of an avalanche of required compositions on abstruse historical and philosophical problems, some of which required as long as seven hours to complete. Even so, the French Ministry of Education remains cavalier. It refuses to lower standards. There is no need to do so. French academic morale remains vigorous; Forestier's students regard him with a mixture of politeness, distance, respect, and admiration. Each year the ministry has more teaching applicants than it can consider. It solves the problem with frugal Gallic reasoning. It simply chooses the best.[18]

NOTES FOR CLASS DISCUSSION

a. What is the author comparing? _____

_____

_____

_____

_____

b. What is the author's point in making the comparison (consider the title of his essay)? Try to state the point in a single sentence.

_____

_____

_____

_____

_____

c. Why do you suppose the author decided not to state his point explicitly? Does he gain an advantage by leading the reader to draw a conclusion rather than stating that conclusion directly?

_____

_____

_____

_____

_____

d. How does the author slant his comparison to favor one side over the other? Consider his choice of words and the kinds of evidence he uses.

_____

_____

_____

_____

_____

2–15 Examining Comparison and Contrast as a Strategy for Essay Development (*RHH*, 2e)

Comparison is often used as the controlling strategy for an entire piece of writing. In the following essay, for example, a student writer organizes her material and develops her point by comparing the medical practices of her great-grandfather, her grandfather, and herself (should she someday become a doctor). Like the writer of the third selection in Exercise 2–14, this writer leaves her point unstated, letting it emerge gradually out of the comparison. Read the essay carefully. Then state its thesis in a sentence or two. Finally, make a detailed outline, showing the specific points of comparison developed in the essay. Use your own paper, and be prepared to discuss your findings in class.

Three Doctors

In 1919, my great-grandfather crossed the rain-swollen Atascosa Creek on horseback to deliver a baby for a desperate farming family trapped by a south-Texas flash flood. He was miles from the small community where he lived, and he carried his sterilized instruments with him in his saddlebags. When he arrived he washed at the backyard pump and delivered the baby with his bare hands; with every bare-handed delivery he risked contracting syphilis. On his way home he made two more housecalls. One was at the home of a friend whose year-old baby suffered from incessant vomiting and diarrhea. He did what he could in a situation that brought back poignant memories. His own daughter died from dehydration at the age of nine months. His last stop was at the home of a man dying with pneumonia.

My great-grandfather did not practice medicine for money; more often than not he was paid with bushel baskets of strawberries, corn, peanuts, and sometimes with chickens, pigs, and calves. He died of a heart attack at age fifty-eight as he leaned over to untie his shoe after a full day's work. He had told no one of his condition. Every store in the county closed its doors in memory of the man who had cared for them.

After World War II, his son, my grandfather, moved his family practice and his family to San Antonio. When he delivered babies he put on rubber gloves, eliminating the risk of syphilis. He delivered babies in a large metropolitan hospital, the Santa Rosa, where he scrubbed for thirty minutes and was covered from head to toe in a surgical gown. If, on a housecall, he found a baby dehydrated from vomiting and diarrhea, he would send him to the hospital and order an intravenous injection immediately. To a patient sick with pneumonia, he would quickly administer anti-biotics. The fondest memory of his fifty-year career was the spontaneous overnight recovery of a man dying of pneumonia after his first phenomenal injection of anti-biotics. Traditionally, my grandfather still accepted bushels of Poteet strawberries from south-Texas patients; however, insead of pigs and calves he accepted services as payment. His patients did carpentry work, upholstery work; they made him a leather coat and they painted his house. The son, like the father, would take care of the whole family—he would counsel them, deliver their babies, take out their tonsils, and nurse their colds. He had an office high up in the Medical Arts Building overlooking the Alamo and took no patients by appointment. They came and brought their needlework and their gossip and waited for hours to see him.

Today the old Medical Arts Building is the posh Emily Morgan Hotel. The Santa Rosa Hospital is the Santa Rosa Medical Center and competes with the South Texas Medical Center with its five hospitals. If I decide to become a doctor like my great-grandfather and my grandfather, I won't choose general practice. Since, like them, I care deeply about other people, I'll choose a specialty like pediatrics or obstetrics. If I choose obstetrics I'll have modern technology to help me deliver the babies. Electrodes attached to mother and baby will monitor vital signs. My patients will rarely die of pneumonia, for I will administer massive doses of antibiotics. I will also have the help of million-dollar machines like the computer tomogram at Methodist Hospital that scans the whole body. In addition, I will be able to order brain scans, bone scans, electrocardiograms, and sonograms. If my grandfather has a heart attack, I will see that he has quadruple by-pass surgery, during which I will see him hooked up to a machine that will pump his blood for him. I will not be paid in pigs or strawberries or services, but the computer in my office will keep track of the mass billing and the records. I will not make housecalls, and Physician's Exchange will screen my midnight calls and preserve my unlisted number.

I will not know my patients as well as my forebears did, and I will have to carry medical malpractice insurance; however, in compensation I will have sophisticated equipment and drugs to help with diagnosis and treatment. Something valuable will be lost, but something valuable will be gained. I will live longer and be able to save more lives. Because of my grandfathers, I will try to preserve, in the midst of enormous impersonality and technology, the values of kindness and caring and compassion—the traditions that have been passed down to me.

2–16 Developing Ideas: Comparison and Contrast (*RHH*, 2e)

Working alone or with a group of classmates, develop details for a comparison/contrast essay. First, name two people, places, things, or ideas that lend themselves to comparison. Then use brainstorming to compile a list of similarities and differences between the two. Finally, study your list and formulate a possible point or thesis that might grow out of the comparison. Possible topics: two musicians, two kinds of food, two sports, two ways of doing something, two holidays, two proposed solutions to a current political or social problem.

Example: Comparison *golf / weightlifting*

Similarities *non-team sports /*
both require mental discipline,
constant practice, and precise
control of body movement . . .

Differences *weightlifting requires*
great physical strength; golf
doesn't / weightlifting year round,
golf in good weather . . .

Possible point of the comparison *Though they seem*
radically different, both weight-
lifting and golf require a high
degree of mental discipline and
physical precision. Contrary to
popular opinion, weightlifting is not
merely a sport of brute strength.

Comparison _____

Similarities _____

_____

_____

_____

_____

_____

_____

_____

_____

_____

Differences_____

_____

_____

_____

_____

_____

_____

_____

Possible point of the comparison_____

_____

_____

_____

_____

2-17 Writing Practice: Comparison and Contrast (*RHH*, 2e)

Write a paragraph, a series of paragraphs, or a complete essay using comparison/contrast as a strategy of analysis. Try one of the following topics, or use one of your own. Use your own paper.

1. Write an essay on the topic you developed in Exercise 2-16. Your essay should make a point. Don't merely compare two items for the sake of

comparison; rather, use the strategy to develop an idea—perhaps the idea you formulated at the end of the exercise.

2. Reread the paragraph in Exercise 2-14 about the size of a basketball court. Write a similar paragraph in which you demonstrate how small (or large) a particular place is by comparing it to another place. Consider the basketball paragraph as a general example, not a detailed model for your paragraph. Possible topics: a dorm room, the interior of a particular car, a handball court, a town.

3. Reread the passage about goats in Exercise 2-14. Write a comical or satirical rejoinder using comparison to show the advantages of the cow over the goat.

4. Reread the student essay in Exercise 2-15. Use some of the methods employed in this essay to develop an essay of your own comparing a business, profession, or other activity as it was practiced in the past to the way it is practiced now. You might start by considering the way your parents' or grandparents' lives differ from yours, or you might consider how your way of doing something has changed in the past several years—for example, writing with pen and paper compared to writing with a word processor.

5. Write a series of paragraphs or a complete essay using comparison as a strategy of analysis. Suggested topics:

Your current attitude toward an issue and your attitude in the past

Two ways of doing something (studying for a test, water skiing, writing a paper, being a parent, eating spaghetti)

Two people, things, activities, or places that appear to be similar but are, in fact, quite different

Two people, things, activities, or places that appear very different but are, in fact, much alike

2-18 Identifying Strategies of Development: Process Analysis (*RHH*, 2f)

Study the use of process analysis in the following passages. Then answer the questions that follow. Be prepared to discuss your answers in class.

1. Like other beers, Coors is produced from barley. Most of the big Midwestern brewers use barley grown in North Dakota and Minnesota.

Coors is the single American brewer to use a Moravian strain, grown under company supervision, on farms in Colorado, Idaho, Wyoming and Montana. At the brewery, the barley is turned into malt by being soaked in water—which must be biologically pure and of a known mineral content—for several days, causing it to sprout and producing a chemical change—breaking down starch into sugar. The malt is toasted, a process that halts the sprouting and determines the color and sweetness (the more the roasting, the darker, more bitter the beer). It is ground into flour and brewed, with more pure water, in huge copper-domed kettles until it is the consistency of oatmeal. Rice and refined starch are added to make mash; solids are strained out, leaving an amber liquid malt extract, which is boiled with hops—the dried cones from the hop vine which add to the bitterness, or tang. The hops are strained, yeast is added, turning the sugar to alcohol, and the beer is aged in huge vats at near-freezing temperatures for almost two months, during which the second fermentation takes place and the liquid becomes carbonated, or bubbly. (Many breweries chemically age their beer to speed up production; Coors people say only naturally aged brew can be called a true "lager.") Next, the beer is filtered through cellulose filters to remove bacteria and finally is pumped into cans, bottles or kegs for shipping.

The most unusual aspect of the Coors process is that the beer is not pasteurized, as all but a half-dozen of the 90 or so American beers are. In the pasteurization process, bottles or cans of beer are passed through a heating unit and then cooled. This destroys the yeast in the brew which could cause spoilage, if the cans or bottles or barrels are unrefrigerated for any long period. However, pasteurization also changes the flavor of beer. Coors stopped pasteurizing its product 18 years ago because it decided that "heat is an enemy of beer," according to a company spokesman.[19]

NOTES FOR CLASS DISCUSSION

a. The author identifies several steps in the "Coors process." Underline the sentences that describe the process. Then number and list the steps below.

_____

_____

_____

_____

_____

_____

_____

_____

b. The first paragraph is largely an objective description of the "Coors process." In making that description, does the author indicate a point or convey an attitude toward her subject? Explain.

_____

_____

_____

_____

_____

_____

_____

_____

c. What is the point of the second paragraph? How is that point linked to the process analysis in the first paragraph?

_____

_____

_____

_____

_____

_____

_____

2.   Every successful gardener knows the importance of a compost heap. Compost—a mixture of partly decayed organic material—is used to fertilize garden soil and to increase its humus content, making nutrients available to plants and improving the earth's ability to hold moisture. Compost is usually made from commonly available plant material found in any yard—grass clippings, leaves, weeds, spent garden plants. Sometimes gardeners buy a few bales of hay or straw to mix into the heap.

My compost heap stands at the corner of a small back-yard garden. I add to the heap throughout the year, but I give it more attention in the fall when the trees lose their leaves and I have on hand a big pile of grass clippings from the summer months.

I begin the compost heap with a layer of twigs and small dead branches. These allow excess moisture to drain from the heap during heavy rains. Next, I alternate layers of different kinds of vegetation. This type of "sandwiching" is necessary to assure that the heap decomposes properly. One layer must contain "carbonaceous" materials (mainly autumn leaves, straw, and dried hay), the other "nitrogenous" materials (mainly grass clippings and spent garden plants). Between layers, I usually toss a light covering of soil. Vegetable peelings and trimmings from the kitchen also go onto the pile as they are available, as do eggshells and coffee grounds. Every few weeks I turn the layers with a pitch fork to keep the pile from matting down. In dry weather, I sprinkle the material with a garden hose to speed up decomposition.

The compost is ready to use when it feels crumbly and has a rich brown color—usually in the spring if the heap was built in the fall. I simply work the compost into the garden soil where it continues to decay, providing nutrients for the flowers and vegetables.*

NOTES FOR CLASS DISCUSSION

a.   Outline the process described in the passage by numbering and listing the steps given.

_____

_____

_____

_____

_____

_____

_____

_____

_____

b. How does the writer manage to avoid making the passage a dry, mechanical recitation of a process? List some of the ways that he achieves a personal tone.

_____

_____

_____

_____

c. What strategies besides process analysis are used in the passage? Explain. _____

_____

_____

_____

2–19 Developing Ideas: Process Analysis (*RHH*, 2f)

Working alone or with a group of classmates, analyze the steps of a process. First, choose a topic by using the "how to" formula illustrated in the example. Then outline the steps needed to complete the process.

Example: Topic___*how to . . . make*___
___*strawberry jam*___

Steps *① select fresh, ripe berries, ② slice them, ③ boil the fruit, ④ add pectin and sugar at the right time ...*

Topic _____

_____

Steps _____

_____

_____

_____

_____

_____

_____

2–20 Writing Practice: Process Analysis (*RHH,* 2f)

Write a paragraph, a series of paragraphs, or a complete essay using process analysis as a strategy of development. Try one of the following topics or use one of your own. Use your own paper.

1. Write a paragraph or series of paragraphs explaining the process you outlined in Exercise 2–19. Include only the essential steps in the process, and make sure that they are presented in clear chronological order.
2. Reread the Coors beer passage in Exercise 2–18. Then visit the reference department of your campus library, and look up the procedure used in some other manufacturing activity—making tires, processing cereal, assembling furniture, bottling soft drinks. Using the Coors passage as a model, describe the steps in the process you studied. (To make your writing more vivid, you might want to observe a "process" first hand at a local factory or business.)
3. Reread the passage in Exercise 2–18 about building a compost heap. Write a similar passage describing a procedure that you know well from

first-hand experience—something you do at work, at home, or as part of a hobby. Assume that your reader is not familiar with the procedure.

4. Write a paragraph, series of paragraphs, or a complete essay that analyzes one of the following:

> The best way to study for an exam, write a term paper, or complete some other academic assignment
>
> The steps to follow in making a major purchase—a car, stereo equipment, a house
>
> A foolproof way to cook something—pancakes, fried eggs, a spectacular dessert (see the strawberry shortcake paragraph in Exercise 6–12, pages 125–126)
>
> The way *not* to do something (try a humorous approach)

2–21 Review Exercise: Identifying Strategies of Analysis (*RHH,* 2a–f)

In the collections of readings used in your composition course or in any other source, locate a brief passage that illustrates each of the following strategies of analysis. (Books, magazines, and newspapers are good possibilities, but don't overlook less obvious sources that you come across every day: pamphlets, cookbooks, advertisements, billboards, menus, even soup can labels and cereal boxes.)

1. Definition (*RHH,* 2a)
2. Division (*RHH,* 2b)
3. Illustration (*RHH,* 2c)
4. Causal Analysis (*RHH,* 2d)
5. Comparison and Contrast (*RHH,* 2e)
6. Process Analysis (*RHH,* 2f)

Transcribe or photocopy your examples and bring them to class for discussion. Be prepared to explain how one of the passages that you found contributes to the overall purpose of the source in which it appears.

2–22 Presenting Evidence for a Claim: Types of Evidence (*RHH,* 2g)

The writers of the following passages use various types of evidence to support claims. In the space after each passage, write a sentence summarizing the main point made in the passage. Then indicate the type(s) of evidence used to support the point: (1) facts and figures, (2) reasoning, (3) citation of authority. Be prepared to discuss the passages in class.

Example: No doubt there are many reasons for the growing teacher shortage in the United States, but Mary Hatwell Futrell, president of the National Education Association, blames the problem primarily on low salaries. The problem is especially acute for newcomers to the profession. According to the NEA, many beginning teachers still earn less than $13,000 a year. In two large Idaho school districts, for example, 1985–86 starting salaries were $12,584 (Boise) and $12,285 (Pocatello). And the national average salary for beginning teachers wasn't much better: $16,500. These figures pale in comparison to beginning salaries for other professionals. According to the College Placement Council and the NEA, accountants start at $20,364; health professionals at $21,360; chemists at $22,764; and computer scientists at $24,984.

Main point *One of the main reasons for the teacher shortage in the U.S. is the low pay for beginning teachers.*

Type(s) of evidence *Citation of authority (NEA President), facts and figures (average salaries)*

1. The assigning of traditional grades (*A* through *F*) in a freshman writing course often works against the purpose of the course—to help students learn to write better. One problem with such grades is that they discourage rather than encourage progress and improvement.

    At the beginning of a writing course, many students earn low grades because they are inexperienced writers. They simply don't know how to write an effective essay, and in the process of learning to do so, they make mistakes—and low grades. Such grades affect the students' confidence and morale, making writing an unpleasant task associated with anxiety and failure. As a result, students are discouraged; instead of working seriously on their writing, they spend time worrying about the easiest way to earn a better grade on the next paper—usually by writing "safe" papers that are simple and correct but lacking in thought.*

Main point _____

_____

_____

Type(s) of evidence _____

_____

_____

_____

2.   The hunter-gatherer tribes that today live like our prehistoric human ancestors consume primarily a vegetable diet supplemented with animal foods. An analysis of 58 societies of modern hunter-gatherers, including the !Kung of southern Africa, revealed that one-half emphasize gathering plant foods, one-third concentrate of fishing, and only one-sixth are primarily hunters. Overall, two-thirds or more of the hunter-gatherer's calories come from plants. Detailed studies of the !Kung by A. S. Truswell, food scientist at the University of London, showed that gathering is a more productive source of food than is hunting. An hour of hunting yields on average about 100 edible calories, whereas an hour of gathering produces 240. Plant foods provide 60 percent to 80 percent of the !Kung diet, and no one goes hungry when the hunt fails. Interestingly, if they escape fatal infections or accidents, these contemporary aborigines live to old ages despite the absence of medical care. They experience no obesity, no middle-aged spread, little dental decay, no high blood pressure, no coronary heart disease, and their blood cholesterol levels are very low (about half that of the average American adult). While no one is suggesting that we return to an aboriginal life style, we certainly could use their eating habits as a model for a healthier diet.[20]

Main point _____

_____

_____

Type(s) of evidence _____

_____

_____

_____

[In the following excerpt from his "Letter from Birmingham Jail," civil rights leader Martin Luther King, Jr., responds to eight of his colleagues, clergymen who criticized his use of civil disobedience as a means of challenging segregation laws. King acknowledges the apparent contradiction in his urging people to obey one law (the 1954 Supreme Court ruling banning segregation in public schools), while at the same time disobeying others (segregation statutes). He attempts to resolve this contradiction by distinguishing between two types of law—just and unjust.]

How does one determine whether a law is just or unjust? A just law is a manmade code that squares with the moral law or the law of God. An unjust law is a code that is out of harmony with the moral law. To put it in the terms of St. Thomas Aquinas: An unjust law is a human law that is not rooted in eternal law and natural law. Any law that uplifts human personality is just. Any law that degrades human personality is unjust. All segregation statutes are unjust because segregation distorts the soul and damages the personality. It gives the segregator a false sense of superiority and the segregated a false sense of inferiority. Segregation, to use the terminology of the Jewish philosopher Martin Buber, substitutes an "I-it" relationship for an "I-thou" relationship and ends up relegating persons to the status of things. Hence, segregation is not only politically, economically, and sociologically unsound, it is morally wrong and sinful. Paul Tillich has said that sin is separation. Is not segregation an existential expression of man's tragic separation, his awful estrangement, his terrible sinfulness? Thus it is that I can urge men to obey the 1954 decision of the Supreme Court, for it is morally right; and I can urge them to disobey segregation ordinances, for they are morally wrong.[21]

Main point _____

_____

_____

_____

Type(s) of evidence _____

_____

_____
_____

2–23 Using Facts and Figures to Support a Claim (*RHH*, 2g)

Write a paragraph in which you state and support a claim by using selected "facts and figures" from the following list. Use your own paper. Possible general topics: Cleveland as a place to locate a new business, Cleveland as a place to shop or live.

FACTS ABOUT CLEVELAND, OHIO

- 250,000 people come in and out of downtown Cleveland each workday.
- 150,000 people work in downtown Cleveland.
- Downtown Cleveland is headquarters for eleven of *Fortune* magazine's top 500 industrial corporations.
- Downtown Cleveland office workers occupy 15 million square feet of space.
- Downtown Cleveland has over 400 retail outlets, including two full service department stores.
- Cleveland's Regional Transit System converges downtown and connects to local and suburban buses.
- Cleveland Hopkins International Airport is twenty minutes from downtown by rapid transit.
- Eleven airlines serve the city.
- Greyhound and Continental Trailways bus terminals are located downtown.
- More than ten colleges and universities are located in Cleveland and nearby suburbs.
- Three major highways (I-90, I-71, I-77) and three railroads serve downtown Cleveland.
- Over 55 percent of the people in the United States live within a 600-mile radius of Cleveland.
- A 424,000-square-foot convention center is located in a seventeen-acre mall in downtown Cleveland.
- The Cleveland area has a 17,000-acre metropolitan park system.

- Cleveland has a symphony orchestra and an art museum.
- Cleveland has professional baseball, basketball, and football teams.[22]

2–24   Using Reasoning to Support a Claim (*RHH*, 2g)

Write a paragraph based on the two premises given below. The paragraph should develop each premise and then end with a logical conclusion. After trying your hand with the sample premises, state two of your own and use them as the basis for another paragraph. Use your own paper.

Premise: Foods heavy in fat, salt, and sugar are unhealthy.
Premise: A particular restaurant or cafeteria serves such food.
Conclusion: ?

2–25   Using Citation of Authority to Support a Claim (*RHH*, 2g)

Write a paragraph in which you make a specific claim about the pressures faced by college students. Include at least one citation of authority to support your claim. The "authority" may be someone you quote from a printed source (check your campus newspaper or do some research in the library) or an expert with first-hand knowledge of the subject—another student or a faculty member you have interviewed. Use your own paper.

2–26   Identifying Points for Concession and Refutation (*RHH*, 2h)

Reprinted below is a portion of an article from *The Chronicle of Higher Education*, a publication read mainly by college professors and administrators. The author, an English professor, argues in favor of required class attendance. Read the passage carefully. Then, working alone or with a group of classmates, make a list of Brown's main points in favor of required attendance. If you were asked to write an essay arguing against a required attendance policy, which of the points on the list would you handle by concession and which by refutation? Make notes to indicate the arguments you might develop in refuting Brown's main ponts. Use your own paper. Be prepared to discuss your ideas in class.

Why I Don't Let Students Cut My Classes
William R. Brown

Last year I announced to my classes my new policy on absences: None would be allowed, except for illness or personal emergency. Even though this violated the statement on cuts in the student handbook, which allows freshmen cuts each term up to twice the number of class meetings per week and imposes no limit for upper-classmen, my students didn't fuss. They didn't fuss even after they discovered, when I telephoned or sent warning notices through the mail to students who had missed classes, that I meant business.

Part of their acceptance of the policy may have resulted from the career orientation of our college, but I don't think that was the main reason. After I explained the policy, most seemed to recognize that it promoted their own academic interests. It was also a requirement that virtually all of them would be obliged to observe—and would expect others to observe—throughout their working lives. It had to be Woody Allen who said that a major part of making it in life is simply showing up.

I told my classes about recent research, by Howard Schuman and others, indicating that academic success is more closely tied to class attendance than to the amount of time spent studying. I shared my sense of disappointment and personal affront when I carefully prepare for a class and a substantial number of students do not attend. I think they got the message that the policy is not arbitrary—that I care about their learning and expect them to care about my professional effort.

I don't claim to have controlled all the variables, but after I instituted the no-cut rule, student performance in my classes improved markedly, not so much in the top rank as at the bottom. In fact, the bottom rank almost disappeared, moving up and swelling the middle range to such an extent that I have reassessed my evaluation methods to differentiate among levels of performance in that range. The implications of so dramatic an improvement are surely worth pondering.

Additional benefits of the policy have been those one would expect to result from a full classroom. Student morale is noticeably higher, as is mine. Discussions are livelier, assignments are generally turned in on time, and very few students miss quizzes.

The mechanics of maintaining the policy kept me a little busier than usual, especially at first, but the results would have justified a lot more effort. I called or mailed notes to several students about their cuts, some more than once. I eventually advised a few with invincibly poor attendance to drop my course, when it seemed that an unhappy outcome was likely. They did.

No doubt this kind of shepherding is easier in a small college. But it can work almost anyplace where a teacher cares enough about the educational stakes to make it work. The crucial element is caring.

* * *

Why do students cut so frequently? I can cite the immediate causes, but I first want to note the enabling circumstance: They cut because they are allowed to. They cut because of the climate of acceptance that comes from our belief that responsibility can be developed only when one is free, free even to act against personal best interests. That that is a misapplied belief in this case can be easily demonstrated. When substantial numbers of students do not attend, classroom learning is depreciated, student and teacher morale suffer, and academic standards are compromised. Students who miss classes unnecessarily are hurting more than themselves. With our complicity, they are undermining what colleges and universities are all about.

Students cut for two general reasons. They have things to do that appear more important than the class, or they wish to avoid what they fear will be painful consequences if they attend. In regard to the first, nursing an illness or attending family weddings or funerals are good excuses for missing a class. But other excuses—the demands of outside jobs, social engagements (including recovering from the night before), completing assignments for other courses—are, at best, questionable.

The other general reason is more disturbing and perhaps less well recognized. A few years ago, I asked several classes what they most disliked about the way courses were taught, and the answer was plain—anything that produced sustained tension or anxiety. I believe cutting is often a result of that aversion. The response of students to feelings of personal inadequacy, fear of humiliation, or a threatening professorial personality or teaching style is often simply to avoid class. This response feeds on itself, as frequent absences make attending even more threatening.

But what accounts for frequent cutting where the teacher tries to make the material interesting, knows the students by name, and approaches them with respect, help, and affability? I accept that question as unanswerable. I simply tell my students: Attend my classes regularly or drop the course. That's the rule.[23]

2–27 Using Refutation in an Argument (*RHH*, 2h)

A. Write a paragraph or two refuting one of the points you identified in the preceding exercise (2–26). First give a fair and objective statement of the point. Then write a reasonable refutation using the notes you developed. Use your own paper.

B. Write an essay supporting or opposing required class attendance on your campus. The author of the article printed in Exercise 2–26 writes as a college professor addressing his colleagues. In your essay, write as a student addressing your classmates. You may wish to concede minor points that count against your argument, but you should meet head-on the strongest objections to your case, handling them through refutation. Take care to state objections fairly before you refute them. Use your own paper.

2–28 Developing an Analogy (*RHH,* 2i)

In a paragraph, develop an analogy using one of the following phrases (or one of your own). Carry the analogy as far as you can, but bring the paragraph to a close before the analogy breaks down or becomes nonsensical.

1. _____ is like going to the dentist.

2. _____ is like a merry-go-round.

3. _____ is like a football game.

4. Eating in the cafeteria is like _____.

5. Choosing a career is like _____.

6. Writing a paper is like _____.

II

COMPOSING WHOLE ESSAYS

3

Developing a Topic and a Thesis

TOPIC

3–1 Review Your Background as a Writer

In order to give yourself and your instructor an overview of your background as a writer, complete the following exercise. Use your own paper.

1. Briefly describe the amount and type of writing you did in your high school courses, especially your English courses.
2. List any college English courses you have taken, and briefly describe the amount and type of writing you did in each one.
3. What type of reading and writing have you done on your own, apart from formal course assignments?
4. List what you consider to be your strengths as a writer.
5. List what you consider to be your weaknesses as a writer.
6. Briefly describe your expectations for this course. What do you hope to accomplish?

7. Drawing on your past experience and your expectations for the future, list the advantages of knowing how to write clearly and persuasively.

3-2 Narrowing a Subject Area to a Topic
(*RHH*, 3a, c)

A. Indicate which five of the following are *subject areas* (SA) and which five are *topics* (T).

Example: The popularity of
Elvis Presley   *T*

The media   *SA*

1. Do computer majors need writing skills?   _____

2. Computers   _____

3. How to raise a show dog   _____

4. News magazines   _____

5. Pressures on college freshmen   _____

6. The Olympic Games   _____

7. Losing weight with a fad diet   _____

8. Dormitory policies   _____

9. High school athletics   _____

10. Raising the drinking age to twenty-one   _____

B. Narrow each of the subject areas in the above list into a *topic*.

Example: the media → television →
television news → television as
a source of national news

1. _____

_____

70

2. _____

_____

3. _____

_____

4. _____

_____

5. _____

_____

3–3 Reviewing Personal Experience (*RHH,* 3e)

In order to establish an inventory of sources for essay topics, review your experience. Name several possible topics for each of the broad categories listed below.

1. early childhood memories _____

_____

_____

_____

2. reading / books _____

_____

_____

_____

3. sports / games / hobbies _____

_____

_____

_____

4. work / skills _____

_____

_____

_____

5. education / school _____

_____

_____

_____

3–4 Reviewing Reading Assignments (*RHH,* 3e)

Review your reading assignments over several days, looking for ideas and opinions that arouse your curiosity or provoke a strong reaction. List five ideas that you might use as writing topics.

1. _____

_____

2. _____

_____

3. _____

_____

4. _____

_____

5. _____

_____

3–5 Freewriting as a Source of Ideas (*RHH,* 3f)

Read the following piece of freewriting, and in the space provided, list two potential topics it suggests to you. Then record the details from the freewriting that might be useful in developing each topic in a three- to four-page paper. Add any other ideas that come to mind.*

Clothing fads. New Wave clothes—earrings, safety pins, sleeveless sweatshirts, kinky sunglasses, strange hair, orange hair, mohawk haircuts. Hair and jewelry are a type of "clothes." Clothes to keep warm, to look good, to create an "image." Clothes as a status sym-
5   bol—preppy clothes, Izod shirts, shirts with little animals on them. Imitation Izod—the Penney fox, and someone has a horse—Polo, I think. Imitation expensive clothes. Designer clothes are a "fad," but they are too expensive for most people, more a status symbol than a fad. People often buy clothes to impress other people or for self im-
10   age—status. Were clothes always status symbols? A good topic for a longer paper with library research. So punk clothes—more an "image" than clothes—or a form of protest. "Clothes as a Form of Social Protest." I probably don't have enough for a paper. Maybe designer clothes, but they're not really a "fad." The cowboy look?
15   It's popular in Texas, but it's more than a fad here. It's always been around. Now *everyone* wants to be a cowboy—boots and hats. Why? Reasons for the cowboy look. How did the fad start? Why do people want the cowboy look? To fit in, status, to impress people, for comfort? Blue jeans are cowboy clothes too—but not just cowboy clothes
20   —a "fad" that's been popular for years. Is it really a fad then? Why do people wear them? Who wears them?—all ages. Different types of jeans—work clothes, casual, and expensive/dressy. My chemistry teacher wears them with a shirt and tie. In "style," but comfortable too and easy to wash and they last for years. Sort of a "national
25   uniform." Jeans as a uniform. Half the people on campus wear them.

Topic 1: _____

Ideas / details _____

_____

_____

_____

Topic 2: _____

Ideas / details _____

_____

3-6 Practice Freewriting (*RHH*, 3f)

Freewrite for ten minutes on one of the following subjects or on a subject of your choice. Then follow the instructions in the preceding exercise as a means of discovering possible topics for a brief essay. Use your own paper.

1. Charity
2. Fast food
3. Bumper stickers
4. Prejudice
5. Advertising

3-7 Brainstorming as a Source of Ideas (*RHH*, 3f)

Look over the following materials (notes from a group brainstorming session). Find several groups of details in the material that suggest essay topics. In the space provided, list two or three of the most promising topics.*

RESPONSIBILITY

Everyone has responsibilities
   —maybe not young children
   —old people?
   —mentally retarded?
   —others?
Parental responsibility
Responsibility of students
   —to parents who pay for education
   —to self
   —to society—pay back benefits gained
Is "duty" same as "responsibility"—"duty to God and country"
Selective service law—responsibility/duty to register at eighteen
Why not women?
Is it more "responsible" to not register?
Obeying the law—duty/responsibility
Thoreau's essay "Civil Disobedience"—duty to follow conscience
    over the law

Does society have responsibilities?
Responsibility for poor, sick, disabled?
—protection/support
—welfare/medicare
Communism—all responsibility taken over by government?
Relationship of responsibility to freedom
Responsibility/duty to vote
Politics and responsibility
Personal responsibility
—relationship between men and women
—marriage
Financial responsiblity
—not paying the rent
—credit cards
—living beyond your means
Taking care of pets
Responsibility in school
Crime and irresponsibility—irresponsible behavior punished?
Capital punishment—government's responsibility to society
What does word "responsibility" mean—check dictionary for origin
of word
Responsibility—other side of freedom?
Essay by Sartre in textbook—man is totally free but also totally
responsible for what he is and does
What does religion say about responsibility?

Possible topics: _____

_____

_____

_____

_____

3–8 Practice Brainstorming (*RHH,* 3f)

Working by yourself or with a group, brainstorm for ten minutes on one of
the following subjects or a subject of your choice. Then use the instructions
provided in the preceding exercise to search for possible essay topics. Use
your own paper.

1. Work
2. Music
3. Happiness
4. Politics
5. Computers

3-9 Using Brainstorming and Freewriting to Explore a Trial Topic (*RHH,* 3f-g)

Formulate a trial topic suitable for a brief essay. Then develop ideas about the topic by *freewriting* or by *brainstorming* with a group of classmates. In the space provided, record several of the most promising ideas.

Trial topic: _____

_____

Ideas: _____

_____

_____

_____

_____

_____

_____

_____

_____

_____

_____

_____

_____

_____

3–10 Asking Reporters' Questions to Explore a Trial Topic (*RHH*, 3g)

Use reporters' questions to explore the trial topic you developed in the preceding exercise (3–9). Write five questions beginning with the words in the following list. Use the questions as a way to probe your topic, to develop further ideas and possibilities.

Example: Topic: The merits of television as a source of national news.

Question: What, *if anything, does television news offer to compensate for its relative lack of depth (e.g., no editorial page, less coverage of "minor" stories)?*

1. Who _____

_____

_____

2. What _____

_____

_____

3. When _____

_____

_____

4. Where _____

_____

_____

5. How _____

_____

_____

6. Why _____

_____

_____

THESIS

3–11 Evaluating Trial Thesis Statements
(*RHH*, 3h)

Evaluate the following trial thesis statements, deciding whether each one contains a single idea that is adequately focused for a three- to four-page essay. In the space provided, briefly justify your answers. If the thesis is adequately focused, explain why; if it lacks focus, jot down suggestions for improving it. (*Reminder:* An adequate trial thesis may contain more than one point, but all points should be subordinate to the one main idea that the writer intends to develop.)

Example: Although television has several advantages as a source of news, a newspaper can offer things that a television program cannot.

Could be better focused – What kind of TV news? PBS? Networks? News specials? What kind of newspaper? What kind of news – national / local? What specifically can a newspaper offer?

1.   I believe that marriage and family development courses in high school should be designed to emphasize the financial situation of the couple, helping them learn to manage a household instead of teaching them about love, sex, and child rearing.

_____

_____

_____

2. The food in Commons cafeteria is bad and should be improved.

_____

_____

_____

3. Congress should institute a national minimum drinking age of twenty-one to help save lives on the highways and to ease problems of law enforcement along state borders.

_____

_____

_____

4. In order to improve our nation's justice system, all prison terms for specific crimes should be fixed by law, and measures should be instituted to limit the drawn-out and expensive court appeals now permitted for those on death row.

_____

_____

_____

5. Most students in the liberal arts believe that a microcomputer would be of little use to them, but owning a computer can make writing papers easier and can give them an edge over the competition in finding a job after graduation.

_____

_____

_____

3–12 Revising Faulty Trial Thesis Statements (*RHH,* 3h–k)

The following trial thesis statements are weak because they fail to propose a definite stand, they use circular reasoning, they beg the question by prejudging an issue, or they are so unreasonably broad that they could not be supported, even in a long essay. In the space provided, indicate why each thesis lacks promise. Then offer a revised version.

Example: Making freshman English a pass/fail course has both advantages and disadvantages.

Problem: *The thesis is wishy-washy. It doesn't take a definite stand.*

Revision: *Making freshman English a pass/fail course would encourage students to concentrate less on grades and more on the gradual improvement of their writing skills.*

1. While some people favor the construction of a high-rise parking garage on campus, others oppose it.

   Problem: _____

   _____

   Revision: _____

   _____

   _____

   _____

2. There are many ways to study for a test.

   Problem: _____

   _____

   Revision: _____

   _____

   _____

   _____

3. The physical education requirement at this college is absolutely useless, and it should be immediately eliminated from the curriculum.

   Problem: _____

   _____

Revision: _____

_____

_____

_____

4. Colleges should have fewer required courses.

Problem: _____

_____

Revision: _____

_____

_____

5. Teachers in college are much different from teachers in high school.

Problem: _____

_____

Revision: _____

_____

_____

3-13 Developing a Trial Thesis (*RHH*, 3h-k)

Using the trial topic and the prewriting material you developed in Exercises 3-9 and 3-10, write a trial thesis statement for a three- to four-page paper. After seeking suggestions for revision from your instructor or a group of classmates, revise the trial thesis.

Trial thesis:_____

_____

_____

Suggestions for revision: _____

_____

Revised trial thesis: _____

3–14 Identifying Faulty Reasoning (*RHH,* 3i–n)

In the following excerpts from student essays and published sources, the writers argue unfairly or illogically. Study the passages for examples of faulty generalizations, either-or reasoning, *post hoc* explanations, exaggerated language, unfair treatment of the opponent, or excessive emotionalism. Be prepared to explain the flaws in reasoning.

1. [A paper arguing for increased U.S. defense spending]

    We must either increase the amount of money we spend on defense or allow the Soviet Union to dominate our nation.*

2. [A paper arguing for decreased U.S. defense spending]

    Politicians who favor more defense spending seem to think that blowing millions of dollars on expensive new weapons will solve all our country's problems.*

3. [A paper arguing in favor of changing freshman English to a pass/fail course]

    If the pressure to earn high grades were removed, students in freshman English would concentrate more on improving their writing skills.*

4. [A newspaper piece about the efforts to raise the drinking age to twenty-one]

    The proposals for increasing the legal drinking age have been brought about due to the increase in [traffic] fatalities in the last decade. Over 250,000 people have died in alcohol-related crashes since the drinking age was lowered.[1]

5. [A letter to an editor]

    Militant feminism is destroying America as the scourge of decency and civility. We have seen an explosion of broken homes, abused children and pornography in the last two decades. Any women who wear pants show their support for our spiritual demise.[2]

6. [An argument against using tobacco addressed to young men; published in 1875]

There is, probably, no tobacco-chewer in the world who would advise a young man to commence this habit. I have never seen a slave of tobacco who did not regret his bondage; yet, against all advice, against nausea and disgust, health and comfort, thousands every year bow the neck to this drug, and consent to wear its repulsive yoke.[3]

7. [An argument against smoking addressed to young women; published in 1898]

Girls sometimes have the idea that a little wildness in a young man is rather to be admired. On one occasion a young woman left a church where she had heard a lecture on the evils of using tobacco, saying, as she went out, "I would not marry a young man if he did not smoke. I think it looks manly, and I don't want a husband who is not a man among men."

Years later, when her three babies died, one after the other, with infantile paralysis, because their father was an inveterate smoker, the habit did not seem to her altogether so admirable. . . .[4]

8. [A 1946 advertisement for Camel cigarettes]

According to a recent nationwide survey: More doctors smoke Camels than any other cigarette.[5]

9. [A 1984 advertisement for Camel cigarettes]

Camel Lights / It's a whole new world.[6]

10. [An argument claiming that popular music is subversive]

In a leading national sex-crazed magazine [*Playboy*], the Beatles, in an exclusive interview, volunteered additional information about their religious convictions, or better, their agnostic-atheistic convictions.[7]

3–15 Analyzing Full Thesis Statements (*RHH,* 3o)

For each of the following full thesis statements, underline the author's main point—the core of the thesis. Then put parentheses around each of the supporting details or reasons that support the main point. Finally, if the author indicates an objection to the main point, enclose it in square brackets.

INSTRUCTIONAL SERVICE CENTER

Example: [Although nightly television news programs give a quick and clear summary of important world news and although they have the advantage of being able to use vivid film footage,] <u>a major daily newspaper is usually a better source of news</u> (because it gives a more comprehensive picture of world events, because it offers a kind of in-depth coverage rarely found on television, and because it can provide perspective and balance through its editorial page.)

1. Being able to plant a vegetable garden is one of the best reasons to rent a house with a back yard instead of living in an apartment because gardening is a relaxing hobby, because it gives the gardener a course in practical botany, because it provides good exercise, and because it costs nothing since it more than pays for itself with the food it supplies.

2. Showing a prize-winning, year-old heifer at a fair involves more than a city person might imagine, including selecting the right calf, feeding and caring for it properly, training it to lead, learning to groom it for the show ring, learning to present it for judging, and caring for and presenting it at the fair itself.

3. While the practice of rotating the location of the Summer Olympic Games benefits the city and country that sponsor the games, the Olympics should be held at a permanent site in order to make the games less political and to place maximum emphasis on the skills of individual athletes.

3–16 Developing a Full Thesis Statement (*RHH*, 3o)

Using the trial thesis you wrote for Exercise 3–13, develop a full thesis statement for a three- to four-page essay. The thesis should state your main point and indicate the major parts of your plan to support that point. Remember that a full thesis statement is a guide to help you gain an overall sense of the essay.

After you have formulated the full thesis statement, seek advice on its effectiveness from your instructor or from a group of classmates. Using the suggestions you gather, revise the thesis.

Full thesis: _____

_____

_____

_____

_____

_____

Suggestions for revision: _____

_____

_____

_____

_____

Revised full thesis: _____

_____

_____

_____

_____

4

Developing a Complete First Draft

4–1 Analyzing a Writer's Voice (*RHH,* 4a)

A. In the following paragraph, the writer's voice is personal. In the space provided, list some of the features that help to establish this voice.[8]

Welcome to English 103, Writing for Business and Industry. My goal in this class is to help you become a better writer of letters, memos, and reports—the kinds of writing you will be doing on the job. Whether you plan to work in business, industry, government, or in another profession, you will probably be asked to write, and the better you can do so, the better your chances of getting the job done, avoiding problems, and advancing in your career.

_____

_____

_____

_____

_____

B. In this passage, the voice is dry and impersonal. Again, list some of the features that help to establish this voice.

> English 103 is entitled Writing for Business and Industry. The primary objective of the course is to improve the student's ability to write correspondence, interoffice memoranda, and technical and professional reports. Obviously, professionals in business, industry, and government benefit if they have skill in written communication. The ability to write means greater productivity on the job and gives the individual greater opportunities for career advancement.

_____

_____

_____

_____

_____

C. Describe a situation in which a writer might want to use each of the voices illustrated in the preceding passages. Which voice would be more effective for an actual course syllabus? Why?

_____

_____

_____

_____

4–2   Using Personal and Impersonal Voice (*RHH,* 4a)

Write two explanatory paragraphs on a topic you know well—anything from fishing to rock music. The first should be a dry, impersonal report. The second, which should include the same·basic information as the first, should be written in a more personal tone, one that is appropriate for a college essay. The second paragraph should grow out of your own interest in the subject and should aim to draw out the readers' interest. Use your own paper.

4–3   Analyzing a Writer's Purpose

Both of the following paragraphs are directed at a general audience of educated readers. The first is an entry from a desk encyclopedia; the second is a paragraph from a popular astronomy book about the origin and development of the universe. Assume in each case that the source contains no other information about the planet Pluto. Keeping in mind the two sources, comment on the likely purpose of each passage. List specfic features of the paragraphs to illustrate how the information and style of writing are matched to the writer's purpose.

1. Pluto, in astronomy, 9th and usually most distant planet from the sun, at a mean distance of 3.67 million mi (5.90 billion km). Because of the high eccentricity (0.250) of its elliptical orbit, Pluto occasionally (e.g., between 1979 and 1999) comes closer than the planet Neptune to the sun. Discovered in 1930 by Clyde Tombaugh, Pluto has an estimated diameter of 1,500 to 2,400 mi (2,400 to 3,800 km) and is thought to have a rocky, silicate core and a thin atmosphere containing methane. Its one known satellite, Charon, was discovered on June 22, 1978, by the American astronomer James Christy. It has a diameter estimated to be about a third that of Pluto.[9]

Purpose: _____

_____

_____

Features: _____

_____

_____

_____

_____

2. Pluto, found in 1930, was the ninth and last planet to be discovered in the solar system. Its orbit is farther from the sun than that of any other planet and probably marks the outer boundary of the solar system. Because Pluto is so far away, we have been able to learn very little about it, except that it appears to be a body similar in size and composition to the earth. It must be a frozen, silent world, far too cold to support any form of life.[10]

Purpose: _____

_____

_____

Features: _____

_____

_____

_____

4-4 Analyzing a Writer's Awareness of Audience

The following passages serve essentially the same purpose: each is the opening paragraph of a book introducing CP/M, an "operating system" used in many home computers. The writer of the first passage, however, makes different assumptions about his audience than does the writer of the second one. In the space provided, briefly describe the audience each writer has in mind, listing specific features that indicate the writer's concept of audience. Keep in mind the length and development of the paragraph, the sentence structure, the vocabulary, and any other features that you consider noteworthy.

1.   The purpose of this chapter is to teach you how to perform basic operations on your computer system using CP/M. No prior knowledge of computers is required. You will first learn the vocabulary and the definitions related to the computer's operation. You will then learn how to turn the computer on, insert your *System Diskette,* and bring CP/M up. You will learn about *files;* how to create them, give them names, and make copies of a file or a complete diskette. You will learn to use the keyboard as well as the screen and the printer to manipulate, display or print the contents of a file. By the end of this chapter, you will have learned how to use all of the most important CP/M commands.[11]

Audience: _____

_____

_____

Features: _____

_____

_____

_____

2. CP/M is a monitor control program for microcomputer system development which uses IBM-compatible flexible disks for backup storage. Using a computer mainframe based upon Intel's 8080 microcomputer, CP/M provides a general environment for program construction, storage, and editing, along with assembly and program check-out facilities. An important feature of CP/M is that it can be easily altered to execute with any computer configuration which uses an Intel 8080 (or Zilog Z-80) Central Processing Unit, and has at least 16K bytes of main memory with up to four IBM-compatible disk drives. A detailed discussion of the modifications required for any particular hardware environment is given in the Digital Research document entitled "CP/M System Alteration Guide." Although the standard Digital Research version operates on a single-density Intel MDS 800, several different hardware manufacturers support their own input-output drivers for CP/M.[12]

Audience: _____

_____

_____

Features: _____

_____

_____

_____

_____

4–5 Adjusting Your Writing for an Audience

In the middle of your first term at college, you find yourself out of spending money. Unfortunately, you failed to budget as carefully as you should have, and several unexpected expenses came up. Using whatever details you choose, write two brief letters requesting a $100 loan. Address the first letter to your parents, the second to the college's financial aid office, which gives short-term student loans for legitimate expenses. Both letters must be convincing, but they should obviously differ in light of the two audiences for which you are writing. After you have finished, list the features of each letter that make it appropriate for the intended audience. Use your own paper.

4–6 Using Your Full Thesis Statement as a Guide to Organization (*RHH,* 4d)

Use the following guide to analyze the full thesis statement that you developed in Exercise 3–16. The material you produce in this exercise should help you organize your essay.

1. In the space below, write the main idea contained in your full thesis statement.

   _____

   _____

   _____

2. Consider possible ways to begin your essay that would draw the reader's interest toward this main point. Write one or two ideas below.

   _____

   _____

   _____

   _____

3. If you are writing an argumentative essay and your full thesis statement indicates an objection you plan to address, write the objection below.

   _____

   _____

   _____

4. Is this the only objection that the reader is likely to raise? List below any other objections you might wish to consider, however briefly, at some point in the essay.

   _____

   _____

_____

_____

_____

5. List below the main points of support included in your full thesis statement. Jot down several details you could use to develop each point.

_____

_____

_____

_____

_____

_____

6. Will any of the points listed in item 5 help you meet the objections listed in items 3 and 4? Which points?

_____

_____

_____

_____

4–7 Developing an Outline for Your Essay (*RHH,* 4e)

Using the material you developed in Exercise 4–6, write either a scratch outline or a subordinated outline for a brief essay. Use your own paper.

4–8 Evaluating a Subordinated Outline (*RHH,* 4e)

Evaluate the following subordinated outline by answering the questions that follow it.

Thesis: A major daily newspaper has several advantages over television news programs as a source of national news.

I. The Advantages of Television News
   A. Nightly television news programs give a clear, concise summary of the day's events.

B. Television has the advantage of immediacy—a vivid, fast-paced presentation using words and film footage.
C. Some people have little time for the news.
D. News anchorpersons can be trusted.

II. The Advantages of a Newspaper
A. Though not as concise, newspapers give a more comprehensive picture of national events.
1. Newspaper coverage is more detailed.

III. Greater Depth of Coverage

IV. Greater Perspective and Balance
A. The editorial/opinion page allows newspapers to provide a range of opinion on national news.
B. Major news is placed in the context of less significant news, giving the reader a better perspective.

1. Does the outline contain enough points for development in a three- to four-page essay? Too few? Too many? Explain.

_____

_____

_____

_____

2. Are the outline categories in logical relation to one another? Explain.

_____

_____

_____

_____

3. Do the points seem to be arranged in an effective order? Explain.

_____

_____

_____

_____

4–9 Revising a Subordinated Outline (*RHH,* 4e)

Revise the outline in the preceding exercise (4–8), eliminating any weaknesses you found. Use your own paper.

4–10 Writing a Scratch Outline (*RHH,* 4e)

Convert the subordinated outline you revised in the preceding exercise (4–9) into a scratch outline. Your outline should indicate the *main* points covered by the subordinated outline. Use your own paper.

4–11 Outlining a Student Essay (*RHH,* 4e)

Study the scratch outline and the student essay printed in Chapter 5 of *The Random House Handbook* (p. 126 and pp. 130–134). Then construct a detailed subordinated outline of the essay. Use your own paper.

4–12 Outlining a Professional Essay (*RHH,* 4e)

In a book, periodical, or the collection of readings used in your composition course, find an essay that you consider well organized. Design a subordinated outline of the essay, showing the arrangement and development of its main points. Use your own paper.

4–13 Writing a First Draft (*RHH,* 4f)

Using the outline you developed in Exercise 4–7, write the first draft of an essay. Keep your audience and purpose in mind, and adopt a voice suitable for the type of essay your are writing. Be prepared to make adjustments as you write, using your outline as a flexible guide, not as an unchangeable blueprint.

5

Revising

5-1 Analyzing a Student's Revisions (*RHH*, 5a–g)

Working by yourself or with a group of classmates, study the following drafts. The one in the left column is the first draft of a student's essay; the one in the right column is the student's revision. Compare the two versions section by section, keeping detailed notes as you work. Use your own paper and the following guidelines.

1. List any conceptual and organizational revisions made by the student, paying close attention to the thesis, the organization, and the development of ideas.
2. List changes in the way the writer begins and ends the essay.
3. List any changes that alter the tone of the essay.
4. List key editorial revisions made by the student: changes in paragraph development; in sentence structure; in word choice; and in grammar, usage, punctuation, and other conventions.
5. List the major strengths of the revised version of the essay.
6. List any remaining flaws in the revised version of the essay, paying attention to minor details that might be changed in order to make the essay more effective.

(*Note:* For a more detailed guide in evaluating the drafts, use the Checklist for Revision in *The Random House Handbook,* pp. 120–121.)

(1)

DRAFT	REVISION
Public schools should be the target of some hard core criticism. After going to public schools for 12 yrs., and entering college, my confidence was blown after discovering that my knowledge of math and English was weak. High school fails in its purpose of preparing a student for college.	High schools often fail in their purpose of preparing students for college because students are too busy learning how to do more important things. In many high schools, the emphasis has shifted from teaching math, English, and the sciences to a much more valuable set of skills. The new breed of high school student is learning to catch a football, play the tuba, or fix a dent in his car. This effort to change the high school curriculum is clearly illustrated at my alma mater, Garfield High School.
Students are not prepared for college because they are too busy learning how to do important things. Rather than taking classes such as trigonometry and writing, students are learning how to run option plays, play the tuba, and fix dents in their car. Emphasis on the football team, band, and vocational programs illustrate how high schools' priorities are all wrong. Most of my high school's attention was focused on football uniforms, a new band hall, and an elaborate vocational program.	

DRAFT	REVISION
This was a wise investment, considering that all the football players learned how to run, throw, and catch, but didn't know what a book looked like. My sophomore geometry class, which contained the quarterback, offensive line, and a few students was taught by coach Ed Alexander. The Football players learned how to loaf in the halls, flirt with the cheerleaders, and ask the coach who he thought was "gonna win the superbowl." Coach never complained if they brought him doughnuts instead of their homework. However, he did buckle down during tests and forced the players to wait until they finished their tests, before they could go to Dunkin' Donut. His peers praised him for how well the players were doing in his class. Students tried to do their work with the help of other students. They were motivated with a 20 point curve. Coaches knowledge of Geometry was limited, so was ours after the year. Coaches class was crowded, so he never really minded if the players left.	During my sophomore year at Garfield I quickly learned that the school's priorities rested on its football team, not on academics. It seems that the faculty and administration were too righteous to allow football players to slack off academically, so they simply made some classes easier for everyone. My geometry class, taught by Coach Ed Alexander and stocked with the quarterback and the offensive line, was one of those classes. If a student didn't have his homework ready for class, he could simply stop at the nearby Dunkin' Donut and pick up a jelly roll to turn in instead. Coach never complained because the process worked smoothly; other teachers praised him for his students' high grades. Coach was a great guy, but his knowledge of geometry was limited, and so was ours at the end of the year.

DRAFT	REVISION
Classes were crowded because money allotted for expansion was used to build a new band hall. The building was a giant, 3 story modern building which made the rest of the campus look like the projects. The rooms needed paint and new desks. Lockers were broken and inoperable, students had to keep their books in their cars to prevent them from being stolen. The cafeteria's long lines and tastey cuisine forced students with enough money and a car to resort to eating out. The parking lots were too small and not paved. Everytime it rained cars would be stuck (or I would have to park 3 blocks away and run to class.) High school doesn't have to be a vacation paradise, but it shouldn't be unbearable.	During my junior year, classes were not only easy, but also crowded because the money originally allotted for more classrooms was mysteriously spent on a new band hall. The school brought in second-hand portable buildings from the nearby Marine Military Academy to accommodate the increased number of students. Air conditioners broke down every two weeks, and left students to bake in the South Texas heat. I never felt bad as long as I knew our band was practicing in a cool, comfortable climate. With all the school's money being spent on the band hall, the rest of the campus became a pitiful sight. The rooms needed paint, trees needed trimming, and the potholes in the parking lot swallowed cars. The penetrating aroma of the school cafeteria was an unpleasant reminder of what laid in store for those brave enough to enter its forbidden doors. The school's environment, overall, was not conducive to education.

DRAFT	REVISION
My senior year I found myself needing only two classes: English & Economics, and was hoping to get into a vocational program which would allow me to get an afternoon job. I assumed that the school would reward me for those hard years of work and let me get out of their way. But, it seems my grades had been too high, and I was not allowed to indulge. I would have been rewarded if I would have flunked out and couldn't read or write. So my senior year was spent productively; I took the two required classes and four useless electives, which made for a thrilling day.	In my senior year, after becoming accustomed to the classes and campus at Garfield High, I was once again dazed by the school's beaurocracy. During registration I discovered that I needed only two classes to graduate. With this in mind, I decided to sign up for the school's highly respected vocational program. Doing so would have allowed me to hold an afternoon job to earn money for the coming year's college expenses. But, upon inspection of my grades, the director of the vocational department refused to admit me: my grades were too high. The school's policy stipulated that only students with a C average or lower could be admitted to the program, since they needed to learn job skills. This policy was meant to help failing students find jobs after they finished high school but it backfired and instead motivated students to do poorly in their classes so that they could enroll in the vocational program.

DRAFT	REVISION
Although these problems were very obvious at GHH, they are shared by other schools. There is no one to blame but the ignorant district taxpayer who allows his money to be spent on a school without any emphasis on education. Because I had lived elsewhere, I knew what a school was supposed to be like. Where would taxpayers hear any complaints? Certainly not from the Football players or the faculty members who valued their jobs. If high schools shifted their priorities to academics, a good education isn't going to hurt any one. Maybe some day students will be prepared for college and not feel bad if they are not on the football team or in the band. Who knows? They might even be able to get into a vocational program.*	The problems at Garfield High were obvious, and they are evident to varying degrees at many other high schools. In Garfield's case, the problems are partly the fault of poorly informed and uninterested taxpayers who have allowed their money to be spent on a school that places little emphasis on academic education. Because classes were easy and students were passing, few people complained. Of course, football players and band members were happy; they were getting a big share of the money. Because I was a transfer student from Richland, Texas, and had attended a different type of school, I knew that there was something wrong at Garfield. If high schools would concentrate more on academics and use football, band, and vocational classes as rewards for good grades, maybe more students would leave high school ready for college, not for a job at McDonald's.*

5–2 Developing a Plan for Revision (*RHH,* 5a–g)

Working by yourself or with a group of classmates, develop a plan for revising the following draft of a student essay. For the first four items listed below, summarize your advice on a sheet of your own paper. For the last item, make notes in the margins of the draft itself.

1. What are the strengths of the essay? Be specific.
2. Is the writer's main idea clear and adequately developed? What improvements could he make?
3. Is the essay organized effectively? How could the organization be improved?
4. Has the writer considered the audience for which the paper was written (his instructor and his classmates)? Should he clarify or delete any material in order to meet their expectations?
5. In the margins of the draft note any editorial revisions that would improve the paper. Consider the following:
   A. paragraph unity, continuity, and development
   B. sentence structure
   C. word choice
   D. errors in grammar and usage
   E. errors in punctuation
   F. errors in spelling

(*Note:* For a more detailed guide in evaluating the essay, use the Checklist for Revision in *The Random House Handbook,* pp. 120–121.)

> I have always thought that organized sports bring out
> the best in a person. Sports demand a great deal of deter-
> mination, which strengthens ones character and developes
> a high standard of moral and social deportment. I learned a
> 5 lot about this during my years as a competitive bicycle
> motocross racer. Although I wasn't a poor sportsman in
> public, but I often revealed to myself signs of being a poor
> loser. My only real competition at National events was my
> arch rival Bob Doran. He lived a couple of miles from me,
> 10 and was the absolute best racer in the thirteen year old
> expert class in the United States.

101

He was sponsored by the Raleigh factory team, and
had countless co-sponsorships from other manufacturers.
He traveled in a huge van with elaborate custom painting,
tauntingly listing his accomplishments on the rear doors.
He was a hero to some, but to me he was very lucky.

At this time I was national number 6, had co-
sponsorships from a few companies, and traveled in my
dads nineteen seventy five chevy suburban with cus-
tome rust. I loathed Bob Doran, not as a person or as a
racer, but because of the way he overshadowed me. I had
beaten him a few times at local races, but they were of
such little consequence, that no one really noticed.
Whenever I lost to Bob I would make excuses, saying to
myself, "If I had all the latest state of the art equipment, I would win to." I even told some people that he
trained in the Soviet Union during the off season and
that his house is filled with the most sophisticated
training equipment from the East Germans. But the simple truth is that he had more natural ability than me,
he would probably always be upstaging me.

Nevertheless, I began training harder than ever for
the world championships which were three months away.
I tried different gearing ratios, and different methods of
gatestarts. I even had my dad videotape a few of my
races, to try and analize my mistakes; but none of this
made me significantly faster. Bob recognized my extra
efforts, he noticed that I was staying closer to him than
ever before. And one night, while we were both practicing under the lights at the local supercross, Bob offered
to help me develope a new technique for speed junmp-
ing, which he guaranteed would take three seconds off

my sprint time. At first I was hesitant, because this guy
was my rival and I couldn't believe that he would help
me, and possibly put himself in jeopardy. But after
45 working with Bob for about an hour I realized that he
actually was trying to help, and it really did take three
seconds off my time. I then realized that I had terribly
misjudged Bob. When I asked him why he had helped
me, he replied, "I need some competition and your the
50 only one who is fast enough." This proved to me that win-
ning isn't everything. Bob and I became the best of friends
and remained competitive, and although he still won the
majority of our races, I never felt bad after a loss.*

5–3 Developing a Plan for Revising Your Own Essay (*RHH,* 5d)

Using the Checklist for Revision on pp. 120–121 of *The Random House Handbook,* develop a plan for revising one of your own drafts, or exchange drafts with a classmate and evaluate each other's work. Make marginal notes to point out specific weaknesses in the essay, and summarize your plan of revision by addressing the first four items listed at the beginning of Exercise 5–2. Use your own paper.

5–4 Evaluating Introductory Paragraphs (*RHH,* 5d)

Evaluate the following introductory paragraphs, deciding how effectively each one catches the reader's interest and announces the writer's topic. Does the paragraph invite you to continue reading the essay? Why or why not? (The brief descriptions are provided to help you evaluate the paragraph's appropriateness for the type of essay it introduces.)

1. [A paper in which a student evaluates her strengths and weaknesses as a writer]

Before I sit down to write a paper, I go through a ritual. I do everything that can be done around the apartment: I do the dishes, clean the bathroom, vacuum the carpet, make the bed, and fix myself something to eat. It is only by doing everything else that I am free to do the one thing I know I must do—my paper.*

2. [A magazine article describing "straight-A illiterates," well-educated people unable to write simply and clearly enough to communicate]

Despite all the current fuss and bother about the extraordinary number of ordinary illiterates who overpopulate our schools, small attention has been given to another kind of illiterate, an illiterate whose plight is, in many ways, more important, because he is more influential. This illiterate may, as often as not, be a university president, but he is typically a Ph.D., a successful professor and textbook author. The person to whom I refer is the straight-A illiterate, and the following is written in an attempt to give him equal time with his widely publicized counterpart.[13]

3. ["Block That Chickenfurter," a magazine article about the ingredients included in hot dogs]

I've often wondered what goes into a hot dog. Now I know and I wish I didn't.[14]

4. [A paper summarizing the first book reviews of George Orwell's *1984*]

In 1949 George Orwell published his anti-utopian novel *1984*. The first critics to read the book had diverse reactions. They disagreed about the book's purpose and criticized Orwell's skills as a novelist. Some were appalled by the picture of the future created in the book, while others praised Orwell for exposing the evils of totalitarianism. Although Orwell confused some reviewers with his style and technique, most critics agreed that his purpose was to illustrate the dangers of political power.*

5. [A paper suggesting a way to improve marriage courses]

In recent years there have been many marriage and family development courses organized on both the high school and college levels. Most of these courses emphasize the emotional relationship of husband and wife; often, they stress the importance of child rearing. Of course, this type of information can be very helpful to the couple in the future, but I believe that the more immediate need for a beginning family is a practical understanding of financial matters. Without the proper management of money, it is difficult for a couple to start out on a solid footing. I believe, therefore, that marriage and family development courses should be designed to emphasize the financial situation of the couple instead of the emotional one.*

5–5 Evaluating Opening Sentences (*RHH,* 5d)

Imagine that you are an instructor reading these opening sentences from student essays on the general topic of education. Decide which sentences make you want to read further and which do not. What is wrong with the sentences that do not? Use your own paper.*

1. As a homemaker returning to school after thirty-two years in the kitchen, I expected the worst, and that is just what I got.

2. In this modern world of ours today, every student has a right to his or her own opinion about education.

3. The new breed of high school student is learning how to catch a football, play the tuba, and fix a dent in his car.

4. Education is an important part of our society.

5. I feel that a college education is a very meaningful experience.

5–6 Writing Opening Sentences (*RHH,* 5d)

For each of the following essay topics, write an opening sentence (or two) designed to catch your reader's attention.

1. Dormitory food

2. A description of a person

3. The advantages of a woman's keeping her own name after marriage

5–7 Finding Effective Introductions (*RHH,* 5d)

Locate three effective introductory paragraphs in magazines, newspapers, or the essay collection used in your composition course. Bring the introductions to class, and be prepared to explain why you selected them.

5–8 Revising an Introductory Paragraph (*RHH*, 5d)

Revise the introductory paragraph from one of your own essays. Bring your revision to class along with the original paragraph, and be prepared to discuss the changes you made.

5–9 Writing a Funnel Opener (*RHH*, 5d)

Write a funnel opening paragraph either for the essay on which you are now working or for one of your earlier essays. Use your own paper.

5–10 Identifying Links between Paragraphs (*RHH*, 5e)

The following passage is a sequence of paragraphs from a much longer essay. Study the passage carefully; then answer these questions:

1. What unifies the passage, making it a self-contained "paragraph block"?
2. What devices does the author use to link each paragraph to the one that comes before it? Circle words and phrases that help establish connections.

Interviewing is one of those skills that you can only get better at. You will never again feel so ill at ease as when you try it for the first time, and probably you'll never feel entirely comfortable prodding another person for answers that he or she may be too shy to reveal, or too inarticulate. But at least half of the skill is mechanical. The rest is instinct—knowing how to make the other person relax, when to push, when to listen, when to stop. And this can all be learned with experience.

The basic tools for an interview are paper and two or three well-sharpened pencils. Is that the most insultingly obvious advice? You'd be surprised how many writers venture forth to stalk their quarry with no pencil, or with one that breaks, or with a pen that doesn't work, and with nothing to write on. "Be prepared" is as apt a motto for the nonfiction writer on his mundane rounds as it is for the Boy Scout alert for the traditional old lady trying to cross the street.

But keep your notebook or paper out of sight until you need it. There's nothing less likely to relax a person than the arrival of someone with a stenographer's pad. Both of you need time to get to know each other. Take a while just to chat, gauging what sort of person you're dealing with, getting him or her to trust you.

Never go into an interview without doing whatever homework you can. If you are interviewing a town official, know his voting record. If it's an actor, know what plays he has been in. You will be resented if you inquire about facts that you could have learned in advance.

Make a list of likely questions—it will save you the vast embarrassment of going dry in mid-interview. Perhaps you won't need it; better questions will occur to you, or the person being interviewed will veer off at an angle you couldn't have foreseen. Here you can only go by intuition. If he strays hopelessly off the subject, drag him back. If you like the new direction, follow him and forget the questions you intended to ask.

Many beginning interviewers are crippled by fear that they are imposing on the other person and have no right to invade his privacy. This fear is almost 100 percent unfounded. Unless the other person is a Howard Hughes, he is delighted that somebody wants to interview him. Most men and women lead lives, if not of quiet desperation, at least of desperate quietness, and they jump at a chance to talk about their work to an outsider who seems eager to listen.

This doesn't necessarily mean that it will go well. In general you will be talking to people who have never been interviewed before, and they will warm to the process awkwardly, self-consciously, perhaps not giving you anything that you can use. Come back another day; it will go better. You will both even begin to enjoy it—proof that you aren't forcing your victim to do something he doesn't really want to.[15]

5–11 Evaluating Concluding Paragraphs (*RHH,* 5f)

Read the essays identified below and evaluate their conclusions. Does each essay end with an appropriate sense of completion? Do the writers succeed in leaving a strong impression of their ideas? Explain. Use your own paper.

1. The student essays on pages 96–100 (Exercise 5–1).
2. The student research essay on pages 324–329 (Exercise 30–6).
3. "Teachers' Tests" on pages 44–45 (Exercise 2–14). This brief essay has no separate concluding paragraph. What gives the essay a sense of completion? Would it be improved by the addition of a formal conclusion? Explain.

5–12 Finding Effective Conclusions (*RHH,* 5f)

Locate three effective concluding paragraphs in magazines, newspapers, or the essay collection used in your composition course. Bring the paragraphs to class, and be prepared to explain why you selected them.

5–13 Revising a Concluding Paragraph (*RHH,* 5f)

Revise the concluding paragraph of one of your own essays. Bring your revision to class along with the original version. Be prepared to explain the changes you made and your reasons for making them.

5–14 Selecting a Title (*RHH,* 5f)

Here are five possible titles for the essay given in Exercise 5-1. Which do you think is the most effective? Justify your choice in the space provided.

1. Why High Schools Are a Failure
2. The Crisis in Our Nation's Schools
3. The New, Improved High School
4. Garfield High
5. Preparing for College: Football or Academics

Your choice: _____

_____

_____

_____

_____

5–15 Proofreading (*RHH,* 5j)

Sharpen your proofreading skills by locating the minor errors in the following passage, the types of errors that often go undetected in final drafts: misspellings, missing letters, apostrophe errors, typographical errors, and punctuation errors. Make the necessary changes in the space above the lines, and circle any punctuation that is not needed. The first paragraph is done for you as an example.

     Michael is a tw*en*ty-four-year-old student, majoring in petro-le*um* engineering. This spring he will complete the requ*ir*ements for his master's degree. He is an attractive and articulate man who speaks with assur*a*nce about his chosen prof*es*sion.

5   Before he began to think of himself as a engineer, Michael had imagine himself as a teacher of the handicaped. While in junier high school, he became freinds, with a boy who had cerebral palsy. Although the boy was Michaels age, mentally and physicaly he was far behind. Moved by the boys handicap, Micheal develop an interest in

108

10   helping those with mental and physical disorders. He was sure that
       apecial education, was the ideal carere for him.

       But in high school he found new freinds and beacme involved in
       atheletics and the Natonal Honor Society. Gradualy he began to turn
       away from special education, and move toward enginering as a
15   career choice. His friends could not beleive that, he actually want to
       teach "retards." They informed him that jobs like that were for
       woman. His teacher's encouraged him to seek a more "challeng-
       ing" proffesion. They said that with his intellectaul ability, he could
       study medicine or science. His parent were proud of his williness to
20   help mentaly retarded people, but they were also "practical." They
       wanted him to chose a proffesion that could offer financial securety.

       Michael is an example of societys steriotyping of mens occupa-
       tional roles. At this piont, he is well established in his field and has
       given up hope of becomeing a teacher of the menally retarded. Yet
25   he still often wonders if he made the write chioce. And he may con-
       tinue to wonder for a long time.*

III

EFFECTIVE
EXPRESSION

6

Paragraphs

6-1 Identifying Paragraph Breaks (*RHH*, 6)

The following passage contains four paragraphs, but they have been printed together without indentations. Decide where the paragraph breaks should be, and explain why.[1]

> The stars within the Galaxy are separated from one another by an average distance of about 36 trillion miles. In order to avoid the frequent repetition of such awkwardly large numbers, astronomical distances are usually expressed in units of the light year. A light year is
> 5 defined as the distance covered in one year by a ray of light, which travels at 186,000 miles per second. The distance turns out to be six trillion miles; hence in these units the average distance between stars in the Galaxy is five light years, and the diameter of the Galaxy is 100,000 light years. In spite of the enormous size of our galaxy, its
> 10 boundaries do not mark the edge of the observable universe. The 200-inch telescope on Mount Palomar has within its range no less than 10 billion other galaxies, each comparable to our own in size and

containing a similar number of stars. The average distance between these galaxies is three million light years. The extent of the visible
15 universe, as it can be seen in the 200-inch telescope, is 20 billion light years. An analogy will help to clarify the meaning of these enormous distances. Let the sun be the size of an orange; on that scale of sizes the earth is a grain of sand circling in orbit around the sun at a distance of 30 feet; the giant planet Jupiter, 11 times larger
20 than the earth, is a cherry pit revolving at a distance of 200 feet or one city block; Saturn is another cherry pit two blocks from the sun; and Pluto, the outermost planet, is still another sand grain at a distance of ten city blocks from the sun. On the same scale the average distance between the stars is 2000 miles. The sun's nearest neighbor,
25 a star called Alpha Centauri, is 1300 miles away. In the space between the sun and its neighbors there is nothing but a thin distribution of hydrogen atoms, forming a vacuum far better than any ever achieved on earth. The Galaxy, on this scale, is a cluster of oranges separated by an average distance of 2000 miles, the entire cluster being
30 ing 20 million miles in diameter.

6–2 Analyzing Paragraph Breaks in a Published Essay (*RHH,* 6)

Select an essay from the collection of reading material used in your composition course (or from another published source). Study the essay carefully to determine the reason for each paragraph break. Be prepared to discuss your findings in class.

6–3 Analyzing Paragraph Breaks in Your Own Writing (*RHH,* 6)

Study one of your own essays. Number the paragraphs, and then write a brief explanation of the reason for each paragraph break. Use your own paper.

6–4 Grouping Sentences into Paragraphs (*RHH,* 6)

Advertisements and newspaper articles are often broken into brief paragraphs designed for ease of reading rather than for grouping ideas. The following advertisement, for example, contains fourteen very brief paragraphs, many only one sentence long. Mark the passage to indicate where paragraph breaks might occur if this were a more traditional piece of writing. Be prepared to justify your choices.[2]

There has always been some friction between smokers and non-smokers. But lately this friction has grown more heated.

The controversy has been fueled by questionable reports which claim that "second-hand smoke" is a cause of serious diseases among non-smokers.

But, in fact, there is little evidence—and certainly nothing which proves scientifically—that cigarette smoke causes disease in non-smokers.

Skeptics might call this the wishful thinking of a tobacco company. But consider the scientific judgment of some of the leading authorities in the field—including outspoken critics of smoking.

For example, in 1983 the organizer of an international conference on environmental tobacco smoke (ETS) summarized the evidence on lung cancer as follows: "An overall evaluation based upon available scientific data leads to the conclusion that an increased risk for non-smokers from ETS exposure has not been established."

Even the chief statistician of the American Cancer Society, Lawrence Garfinkel, has gone on record as saying, "passive smoking may be a political matter, but it is not a main issue in terms of health policy."

Which brings us back to our original point: cigarette smoke can be very annoying to non-smokers.

But how shall we as a society deal with this problem?

Confrontation? Segregation? Legislation?

No. We think annoyance is neither a governmental problem nor a medical problem. It's a people problem.

Smokers and non-smokers have to talk to one another. Not yell, preach, threaten, badger or bully. Talk.

Smokers can help by being more considerate and responsible. Non-smokers can help by being more tolerant. And both groups can help by showing more respect for each other's rights and feelings.

But eliminating rumor and rhetoric will help most of all.

Because when you stick to the facts, it's a lot easier to deal with the friction.

PARAGRAPH UNITY

6–5 Recognizing Paragraph Unity (*RHH*, 6a)

Underline the main sentence in each of the following paragraphs—the sentence that states the central point developed in the rest of the paragraph. Then decide if each paragraph is unified. If not, identify the problem by circling any material that is not clearly related to the central point. In the space provided, briefly explain the problem.

Example: I had always assumed that when I finished my degree in Computer Information Systems, I would get a job and do exactly what I had been trained to do—write programs. I discovered, however, that this was a false assumption. During my junior year I took a computer course in which the professor told the class that writing is often an essential part of a programmer's job. Programmers, he explained, must keep logs, fill out reports, and carefully document the programs they write. In fact, documentation is an essential part of the job because it enables an employer or co-worker to understand what the programmer has done. Most computer majors have little time for electives because their degree programs require so many courses in computer science. When they do take electives, technical subjects usually win out over subjects like English.*

After two introductory sentences, the paragraph develops its main point—on-the-job writing for programmers. Then the paragraph shifts to a new point—electives taken by computer majors.

1. Many professional musicians complain that the violins, cellos, and other string instruments produced today cannot match those crafted at the close of the Renaissance by a group of Italians working in the city of Cremona. The sound from many modern instruments has an unpleasant edge when certain notes are played, similar to the effect of a hundred violins all playing the same note with one ever so slightly out of tune. In addition, most of today's instruments are not well balanced—some

116

notes are richer and more resonant than others—and their sound does not carry as well as that from a Cremonese instrument. Violins are today made throughout the world; no single country or community has cornered the market on fine instrument making.[3]

---

2. For thousands of years human beings have communicated with one another first in the language of dress. Long before I am near enough to talk to you on the street, in a meeting, or at a party, you announce your sex, age and class to me through what you are wearing—and very possibly give me important information (or misinformation) as to your occupation, origin, personality, opinions, tastes, sexual desires and current mood. I may not be able to put what I observe into words, but I register the information unconsciously; and you simultaneously do the same for me. By the time we meet and converse we have already spoken to each other in an older and more universal tongue.[4]

---

3. The social weaver is a superlative bird architect, and flocks of birds build enormous "apartment house" nests in the flat-topped acacia trees of the South African veldt. The American Museum of Natural History has thousands of nests in its collections and vaults. Crafted out of coarse grass and twigs, weavers' nests are not woven but thatched like a haycock. The result is a large, hanging mass of straw whose underside is perforated by the entrances to individual nests. Every year the flock adds to the nest,

and sometimes the weight of the nest will cause the supporting branches to collapse. Nests have been observed in use over 100 years, and the very largest can reach almost 2,000 cubic feet in volume.[5]

---

4. Since I had been away at college for only a month, I expected everything to be the same when I made my first visit home. But to my surprise, a considerable amount of change had occurred. My sister had taken little time in moving into my room, which included not only a large bed but also my television. And because my parents had turned my sister's room into a study for their use, I had to stay in the guest room. I had expected this to happen, of course, but I was surprised at the quickness with which it was done. Although more happened than I had anticipated, the family atmosphere itself remained the same. When I first arrived, there were the usual "hellos" and questions about college life. And after a good meal and several hours of talk, everything settled back into a comfortable routine.*

---

5. More than three centuries after the Indians first showed Captain John Smith how to grow it, pumpkin is still regarded as an incredibly versatile ingredient. You can wake up to a plate of pumpkin pancakes or pumpkin muffins spread with tangy pumpkin preserves. Or follow a dinner of pork with pumpkin sauce with a slice of mouth-watering pumpkin apricot brandy pound cake or pumpkin cheesecake. It's little

wonder that in 1683 a Colonist rhymed: "We had pumpkins in the morning and pumpkins at noon. If it were not for pumpkins, we'd be undone soon."[6]

6-6 Supplying Main Sentences (*RHH,* 6a)

The following paragraphs lack explicit main sentences. For each one, write a sentence that sums up the point developed in the paragraph. Is the paragraph more or less effective with its central point explicitly stated? Why?

1. At Halloween, children bob for apples and find them nestled in their "trick-or-treat" bags among the candy and popcorn balls. At Thanksgiving, grade schoolers make turkeys from apples rigged with pipe cleaners, paper cutouts, and marshmallows. During the summer months, every child looks forward to eating a sticky candied apple while walking down the carnival midway. And when fall rolls around, good boys and girls everywhere present their teachers with polished red apples, the traditional academic offering.*

   Main Sentence: _____

   _____

2. The roof of the house sagged in several places, the ceilings were badly stained where water had leaked in over the years, and the walls were bare in a dozen places where the paper had peeled away from the slatted wood. In the kitchen, nearly half the tile was off the wall behind the sink, and the countertops badly needed regrouting. Hardwood boards popped up everywhere, squeaking and groaning as we walked over them. In one spot the floor was rotted away by years of moisture that had seeped in around an old chimney pipe that ran from the basement up through the roof.*

   Main Sentence: _____

   _____

3. The familiar *slip joint pliers* are named for the two-position pivot that provides both normal and wide jaw openings. Broad-jawed *lineman's pliers* have side cutters which equip them for heavy-duty wire cutting and splicing. *Channel-type pliers* with multiposition pivots adjust for

jaw openings up to 2 inches and will grip any shape. *Long-nosed pliers* are used to shape wire and thin metal, and often for cutting as well. *Diagonal-cutting pliers* have no gripping jaws and are used for cutting only. Also for cutting only are *end cutting nippers,* which can snip wire, small nails, and brads.[7]

Main Sentence: _____

_____

6–7 Selecting Details for a Unified Paragraph (*RHH,* 6a)

This exercise contains a list of factual statements about elephants. Use appropriate details from the list to write a paragraph on one of the suggested topics. Underline your main sentence. Some of the information may be relevant for either paragraph. Feel free to add details that are not in the list.[8]

Topic 1: The elephant as an endangered species

Topic 2: Humankind's use of the elephant

1. People have trained Asiatic elephants for thousands of years.

2. Because of their size and inefficient digestion, elephants require enormous amounts of food.

3. For more than a thousand years, hunters have killed African elephants for their ivory tusks.

4. Laws now forbid the killing of elephants for ivory.

5. There may now be fewer than 1,300,000 elephants in Africa and fewer than 25,000 in Asia.

6. Elephants are used today in southern Asia as work animals.

7. A dwindling food supply is an even greater threat to the elephant than are ivory hunters.

8. Before the invention of heavy machinery, elephants were the most powerful force available to humans for pushing and carrying objects.

9. Humans are taking over more and more of the land in Africa and Asia—land once used by elephants for feeding.

10. Today elephants are used to help clear forests and to do other heavy labor.

11. The price of ivory today is extraordinary; a single pair of tusks may sell for more than $20,000.

12. Elephants have been used in circuses for at least 2,000 years.

13. Some zoos regularly feature elephant rides.

14. Poachers continue to kill elephants for their tusks.

15. We may always be able to see elephants in zoos, but will they survive in the wild?

6–8 Writing a Practice Paragraph (*RHH,* 6a)

Write a unified paragraph, beginning either with one of the following main sentences or with a main sentence of your own.

1. A good tennis player (or any other athlete) must have a disciplined mind as well as a disciplined body.

2. Living in a dorm room (or an apartment) is much easier (or more difficult) than I thought it would be.

3. If I could spend one hour talking to a famous person from history, I would choose . . .

4. If high schools want to better prepare students for college, they should . . .

5. When we went to clean up the next day, we found that the room had been devastated by the all-night party.

PARAGRAPH CONTINUITY

6–9 Paragraph Continuity: Responding to a Previous Sentence (*RHH,* 6b)

Assume that each sentence given below is the first sentence in a paragraph. Write two sentences that could follow it—one a sentence of illustration, the other a sentence of limitation.

Example: Ludwig almost always prefers ballroom dancing.

Illustration: *Last week he refused to go out unless we all agreed to foxtrot.*

Limitation: *But on a rare occasion he kicks loose and does some break dancing.*

1. In the past year the local animal shelter picked up more than three hundred dogs and cats.

    Illustration: _____

    _____

    Limitation: _____

    _____

2. In the cafeteria last Thursday I ate one of the best meals I've ever had.

    Illustration: _____

    _____

    Limitation: _____

    _____

3. Most television programming today is designed to appeal to twelve-year-olds.

    Illustration: _____

    _____

    Limitation: _____

    _____

4. Smoking ought to be banned entirely on commercial airplanes.

    Illustration: _____

    _____

    Limitation: _____

    _____

5. My brother told me that I was crazy to buy this old wreck of a car.

Illustration: _____

_____

Limitation: _____

_____

6–10 Recognizing Paragraph Continuity (*RHH,* 6b–e)

In the following paragraphs, circle the words and phrases that contribute to paragraph continuity. Then, in the space provided, explain briefly the main method(s) used by the writer to achieve continuity: (1) signal words and phrases, (2) pronouns, (3) repeated key words and phrases, (4) repeated sentence structure.

Example: (Fannie) was the worldliest old (woman) to be imagined. (She) could do whatever (her) hands were doing without having to stop talking; and (she) could speak in a wonderfully derogatory way with any number of pins stuck in (her) mouth. (Her) hands steadied me like claws as (she) stumped on (her) knees around me, tacking me together. The gist of (her) tale would be lost on me, but (Fannie) didn't bother about the ear (she) was telling it to; (she) just liked telling. (She) was like an author. In fact, for a good deal of what (she) said, I daresay (she) *was* the author.[9]

The main device is the repeated use of pronouns to refer to Fannie.

1. If motherhood isn't instinctive, when and why, then, was the Motherhood Myth born? Until recently, the entire question of maternal motivation was academic. Sex, like it or not, meant babies. Not that there haven't always been a lot of interesting contraceptive tries. But until the creation of the diaphragm in the 1880's, the birth of babies was largely unavoidable. And, generally speaking, nobody really seemed to mind.

For one thing, people tend to be sort of good sports about what seems to be inevitable. For another, in the past, the population needed beefing up. Mortality rates were high, and agricultural cultures, particularly, have always needed children to help out. So because it "just happened" and because it was needed, motherhood was assumed to be innate.[10]

2. When my dad comes through the door at the end of the day, he has only two things on his mind: a cold beer and a hot meal. His straw hat is the first thing to go before he washes his callused hands and heads for the kitchen. During supper he wears the same worn-out boots he's had for years. His cotton shirt is still new, but his blue jeans, patched on both knees, would make better rags than pants. His tanned skin is leathered from too much sun, his strong arms hardened from throwing calves and building fences. And his legs are bowed to fit the saddle he uses every day. Work and age have started to gray the tips of his hair.*

3. An elephant is a bawling baby squeezed under its mother's belly as a dozen older relatives surround the pair, facing out in defense against an approaching lion. An elephant is a frisky adolescent ripping up hundred-year-old trees and flinging them about. An elephant is 20,000 pounds sliding down a muddy bank, splashing into a river, and totally submerging itself until a fleshy snorkel breaks the waves for air. And an elephant is a lonely wanderer, happening upon the bones of a long-dead elephant and stopping for half an hour to trace the bleached forms gently with its trunk.[11]

4. Like the other degenerative diseases, heart disease is ordinarily present for a long time in the body before drastic symptoms appear. In fact, in our country, heart disease often begins in the early twenties, growing worse as the years pass until finally the inevitable heart attack strikes. For most people the first heart attack does not come until the fifties or sixties. But for thousands of people every year, the first heart attack comes in the twenties. Occasionally even a person in his teens may experience a fatal heart attack.[12]

6–11   Recognizing Paragraph Continuity (*RHH,* 6b–e)

Take a paragraph from one of your textbooks or from another published source and photocopy it or write it out on your own paper. Then circle the words and phrases that contribute to continuity. Look for explicit signal words as well as pronouns or repeated words that help the writer link ideas into a coherent pattern.

6–12   Revising for Paragraph Continuity (*RHH,* 6b–e)

Revise the following paragraph to improve its continuity. Add signal words and phrases where appropriate to strengthen connections between sentences. Underline the transitions you include. Use your own paper.

Anyone can make strawberry shortcake. Take one of those spongy, little store-bought "cakes" (they come six to a package), fill the indentation with a spoonful of strawberries (thaw them first), and plop on a dab of Cool Whip. If you want to make the real thing, you have to do some work. Make the shortcake from scratch—not the spongy kind, but a good drop biscuit dough with plenty of sugar thrown in. Pour on the strawberries (don't be stingy)—fresh, ripe, sliced thin, sprinkled with sugar, and left to stand for at least three hours. Put a big scoop of natural vanilla ice cream on top. (Homemade is best; if it's not available, use only the finest commercial brand.) Crown the whole thing with a thick mound of freshly whipped cream. *That* is strawberry shortcake.*

6–13 Review Exercises: Peer Editing for Paragraph Unity and Continuity (*RHH,* 6a–e)

Bring to class a rough draft of your current essay. Exchange papers with a classmate, and carefully check each other's work for paragraph unity and continuity. Use the following guidelines:

1. *Unity.* Underline any material that does not belong in a particular paragraph; then write a brief two- or three-sentence note explaining why you underlined the material.
2. *Continuity within Paragraphs.* Note in the margins any paragraph that lacks continuity; point specifically to places where transitional expressions or repeated words could improve the links between sentences.
3. *Links between Paragraphs.* Check the transitions between paragraphs. Note in the margins any places where one paragraph could be linked more effectively to another.

If your classmate points out any paragraphs in your essay that lack unity or continuity, revise them before submitting the final copy.

DEVELOPMENT

6–14 Recognizing Patterns of Paragraph Development (*RHH,* 6f–h)

In the space provided, identify the method of development used in each paragraph—direct, pivoting, or suspended. Then underline the main (or topic) sentence, and indicate with a bracket which sentences, if any, "limit" the main point and which "support" it. (*Note:* The final paragraph lacks an explicit main sentence. In the space provided, write a sentence that sums up the paragraph. Why did the writer not include such a sentence?)

Example: | As a poet, W. H. Auden has always had his share of detrac-
tors, first in the 1930's with the negative response to his work in
the influential journal *Scrutiny,* and later in two articles by Ran-
dall Jarrell criticizing various ideological changes in his poetry.
Limit | Even today some argue that Auden's work is uneven or that it
represents a serious decline from the brilliance he demonstrated
in the 1930's. Despite all this, however, Auden is generally
regarded today as one of the major poets of the twentieth century.
Support | Several of his poems are well established as standard anthology
pieces and his work as a whole is recognized for its impressive
range of thought and its technical brilliance.[13]

Pivoting Paragraph

1.   The fighting bull is to the domestic bull as the wolf is to the dog. A
domestic bull may be evil tempered and vicious as a dog may be mean
and dangerous, but he will never have the speed, the quality of muscle
and sinew and the peculiar build of the fighting bull any more than the
dog will have the sinews of the wolf, his cunning and his width of jaw.
Bulls for the ring are wild animals. They are bred from a strain that
comes down in direct descent from the wild bulls that ranged over the
Peninsula and they are bred on ranches with thousands of acres of range
where they live as free ranging animals. The contacts with men of the
bulls that are to appear in the ring are held to the absolute minimum.[14]

2.   I do not believe that the dorm visitation hours on school nights
should be extended to midnight. It is true that college students are
mature enough to regulate their own lives, and, indeed, there are sev-

eral good reasons for extending the hours to midnight. But finally, the very nature of dorm life makes the earlier hours preferable. For one thing, some students do most of their studying late at night, and visitors on the floor inevitably disrupt their work. An occasional late visitor would be fine, but with dozens of people living together, a visitor is likely to be on the floor nearly every night. Security is another good reason for the 10:00 P.M. curfew. In the past month several prowlers have been reported in the dorm. One room was cleaned out by thieves— at 11:00 P.M. on a Tuesday. Earlier visitation hours won't solve such problems, but they will make it easier to keep out unwanted visitors late at night after many dorm residents are asleep.*

---

3.   In normal life the woodchuck's temperature, though fluctuant, averages about 97 degrees. Now, as he lies tight-curled in a ball with the winter sleep stealing over him, this body heat drops ten degrees, twenty degrees, thirty. Finally, by the time the snow is on the ground and the woodchuck's winter dormancy has become complete, his temperature is only 38 or 40. With the falling of the body heat there is a slowing of his heartbeat and his respiration. In normal life he breathes thirty or forty times each minute; when he is excited, as many as a hundred times. Now he breathes slower and slower—ten times a minute, five times a minute, once a minute, and at last only ten or twelve times in an hour. His heartbeat is a twentieth of normal. He has entered fully into the oblivion of hibernation.[15]

---

4.   Family life has a good deal to do with the development of a child's ability to understand, to use, and to enjoy language. It strongly influ-

ences his impression of the value of reading, and his confidence in his intelligence and academic abilities. But regardless of what the child brings from home to school, the most important influence on his ability to read once he is in class is how his teacher presents reading and literature. If the teacher can make reading interesting and enjoyable, then the exertions required to learn how will seem worthwhile.[16]

---

5.   In Athens, women had no more political or legal rights than slaves; throughout their lives they were subject to the absolute authority of their male next-of-kin. They received no formal education, were condemned to spend most of their time in the women's quarters of their home, and were subject to arranged marriages. A wife seldom dined with her husband—and never if he had guests—and on the rare occasions that she went out of doors, was invariably chaperoned; it was illegal for her to take with her more than three articles of clothing, an obol's worth of food and drink (in today's terms, a sandwich and a glass of milk), and if she went out after dark she had to go in a carriage with a lighted lantern.[17]

---

6.   There are circumstances where the otherwise absolute obligation of the law is tempered by exceptions for individual conscience. As in the case of the conscientious objector to military service, the exception may be recognized by statute or, as in the case of the flag salute for school children, it may be required by the First Amendment. But in countless other situations the fact that conscience counsels violation of the law can be no defense. Those are the situations in which the citizen is placed

in the dilemma of being forced to choose between violating the dictates of his conscience or violating the command of positive law.[18]

---

7.   My job as a blood bank laboratory technician occasionally has its lighter moments. One day our shipping department decided to have some fun with us. Late that afternoon they brought a small, unusually labeled box into the laboratory. On the box were several stickers that read, "Caution!" "Handle with Care!" and "Biohazard!" After eyeballing the box from a distance for some time, I walked up and cautiously opened it. Inside, among shredded newspaper and foam rubber, was a single pint of green liquid. Quickly, I snatched up the invoice and read, "Enclosed: One pint of rare type O witches' blood." For the first time that day I realized the date—October 31.*

---

8.   On a cold, snowy evening Kevin and I left Seattle bound for home, a three-day, nonstop drive back to Texas through some of the most beautiful country I know. That night I started the first driving shift on slick, snow-covered roads. As I was driving up the mountains, just outside Seattle, my headlights shone on a figure in the road that appeared to be a horse. I started slowing down, trying to figure out just what it was. Just then Kevin said, "It's a big buck!" I stopped the truck about twenty feet in front of him—the biggest deer I'd ever seen. He just stood there, blinded by the headlights, breathing frosted clouds of air from his nose. He looked proud and beautiful standing there with snow on his antlers and a look of fury in his eyes. We got out for a closer look, but as we did, he took off, hardly making a sound. I remembered looking into his eyes all the way home.*

6-15 Writing Practice Paragraphs: Patterns of Development (*RHH,* 6f–h)

Write three paragraphs—one using *direct* development, one *pivoting,* and one *suspended.* Draw your topics from the following list or, if you wish, design your own topic. Use your own paper.

1. A description of a person, place, or incident
2. The excessive emphasis on athletics in high school
3. The importance of athletics in high school
4. The content of an ideal marriage course
5. Food in the dormitory or at a specific restaurant

6-16 Revising a Choppy Paragraph (*RHH,* 6i)

The following paragraphs are choppy—they provide too little information to support the writer's point. Working alone or with a group, revise the first two paragraphs, adding as much detail as necessary to achieve adequate development. For the third item—a series of choppy paragraphs—you may either rearrange or delete some of the information in order to give the resulting paragraph an adequate focus. Use your own paper.*

1. Most students today attend college in order to get jobs when they graduate. Because of this interest in careers, students major in fields that offer the best job opportunities. Fields of study that do not lead directly to jobs are not as popular as they once were.

2. Mr. Mahon's yard was the envy of the neighborhood. His grass was always thick and neatly trimmed. In the front of his house was a beautiful garden of climbing roses.

3. Most people consider charity an obligation. They give a few dollars at church every week or they make donations elsewhere.

   People often seem to be more concerned about tax donations for charity than about the charity itself.

   Few people are willing to give up their own time for a charitable purpose. It is easier to write a check.

6-17 Revising a Bloated Paragraph (*RHH,* 6i)

The following paragraph is poorly developed because it contains too much information without an adequate focus. Working alone or with a group, revise the paragraph, deleting irrelevant material and focusing the paragraph on a single idea. If you prefer, you may change the passage into a series of paragraphs, each one developing a point contained in the original bloated paragraph. Use your own paper.

When I write a paper, I usually type out a complete first draft, triple-spaced. I then revise it by handwriting changes in the margins and between the lines. I often spend an hour or more making changes right on the typed draft. When my paper is a barely readable maze of
5   cross-outs, arrows, inserts, and marginal notes, I usually decide to quit revising. I then type a final copy from my marked-up draft, sometimes making additional minor changes as I type. I have always written this way, and I suppose I always will; the method has become a comfortable habit. I find it hard to pinpoint my specific strengths
10   and weaknesses as a writer, partly because I lack objectivity about my work. I think I have a good attitude toward writing, better than I used to have, but I do have a hard time writing for a specific audience. When I write a paper, I simply write; I rarely think about gearing my work for a specific reader, and sometimes this leads to problems.
15   Some would consider my procrastination a weakness, but I consider it a strength. Putting off a writing project until near the deadline helps me concentrate on my subject and focus my energy. My method of writing is also very efficient. Since I limit my drafting and revising to a single copy of the paper, I spend much less time recopying
20   than most people do. Once my heavily edited first draft is finished, I go straight to the typewriter.*

6-18 Review Exercise: Peer Editing
for Paragraph Development (*RHH,* 6i)

Bring to class a rough draft of your current essay. Exchange papers with a classmate, and carefully check each other's work for adequate paragraph development. Use the following guidelines:

1. *Well-Developed Paragraphs.* Put a check in the margin next to any paragraph that you consider especially well developed.

2. *Choppy Paragraphs.* Identify any paragraph that needs further development; make specific suggestions for revision, writing your advice in the margins or on a separate sheet of paper.
3. *Bloated Paragraphs.* Identify any paragraph that contains too much information without an adequate focus; make specific suggestions for revision, writing your advice in the margins or on a separate sheet of paper.

If your classmate points out any paragraphs in your essay that need improvement, revise them before submitting the final copy.

7

Sentences

7-1 Identifying Main Ideas (*RHH*, 7a)

Underline the main idea of each sentence in the following passage. If a sentence contains two main ideas joined by a coordinating conjunction, circle the conjunction. The first sentence is done for you as an example.

When Nixon agreed to debate Kennedy in a series of national telecasts, <u>the Vice President and his lieutenants were certain that Nixon would enhance his advantage.</u> The Vice President had used the medium to good effect in 1952, and he could now count on a phenom-

5   enally large audience. In the 1950s the number of American families who owned television sets had risen from 4.4 million to 40 million, 88 per cent of the nation's families. Millions of Americans—estimates ran as high as 70 million—tuned in to watch the first contest.

The outcome was a major surprise. While Nixon seemed con-
10 stantly on the defensive, obsessed with scoring debater's points
against his rival, Kennedy ignored the Vice President and spoke
directly to the nation, enunciating his major theme of national purpose: "I think it's time America started moving again." While Kennedy appeared calm and self-possessed, Nixon seemed tense and
15 haggard (TV cameras were unkind to his features).

Although three more debates followed, they were largely unil-
luminating encounters in which various issues were so fuzzed over
that neither man's position was distinct; it was the first debate that
made its mark and, many thought, determined the outcome of the
20 election. Almost all observers agreed that Kennedy had scored a
clear triumph; at the very least, he had drawn even with Nixon and
could no longer be dismissed as a callow upstart.[19]

7–2 Identifying Main Ideas
In Your Own Writing (*RHH,* 7a)

Photocopy or write out a page from one of your essays. Then underline the
main idea in each sentence. Use your own paper.

7–3 Selecting Sentences with Clear Main Ideas
(*RHH,* 7a–b)

Circle the subjects and verbs in the following sentences; then decide which
sentence in each pair has a clearer main idea—a stronger alignment between
meaning and grammatically important words. Circle the letter of the sentence
you choose.

Example: (a) There was agreement by the candidates to answer

all questions.

(b) The candidates agreed to answer all questions.

135

1. (a) Our expectation was to finish the job in three months.

    (b) We expected to finish the job in three months.

2. (a) A report from the Commission on Central America received study by the president.

    (b) The president studied a report from the Commission on Central America.

3. (a) After receiving complaints from several people, the FBI investigated Bilko's mail-order division.

    (b) An investigation of Bilko's mail-order division was initiated after the FBI received complaints from several people.

4. (a) The senator voted against the bill because he believed that the dairy industry was already burdened by needless government regulation.

    (b) The reason for the senator's negative vote in regard to the bill was his belief that the dairy industry was already burdened by needless government regulation.

5. (a) The hiring of unskilled workers to fill the positions necessitates an investigation by the agency.

    (b) The agency must find out why unskilled workers were hired to fill the positions.

7–4 Revising Sentences to Align Meaning with Subjects and Verbs (*RHH,* 7a–f)

Revise the following sentences to clarify main ideas. For sentences 1–5, use the underlined word to form the subject. Your goal should be to make each sentence as readable as possible.

Example: The use of computers is now increasing in many <u>professional</u> fields.

Today, more and more professionals use computers.

1. A presidential warning was issued in order to stop further news leaks at the Justice Department.

   _____

   _____

2. Humans are sometimes attacked and eaten by lions that are too old to attack their usual prey.

   _____

   _____

3. The main type of music played by the group is bluegrass music.

   _____

   _____

4. The change to a later time for our second meeting was thought to be necessary because the first meeting, which was held early, was poorly attended. [Change *our* to *we.*]

   _____

   _____

   _____

5. The thing that should be of most concern to instructors is that students sometimes are unable to synthesize the many facts they are given in courses.

   _____

   _____

   _____

For sentences 6–10, convert the underlined noun into the main verb of the sentence. Make any other changes necessary to clarify main ideas.

Example: The filing of legal proceedings against the dog's owner occurred after Patrick was attacked.

After he was attacked by the dog, Patrick filed a lawsuit against its owner.

6. I finally reached an <u>understanding</u> of the point being made by the lecturer.

_____

_____

7. The <u>discovery</u> of how to make cheese occurred thousands of years ago in human history.

_____

_____

8. <u>Revisions</u> of departmental policy occur at the director's level.

_____

_____

9. A <u>need</u> exists for the university to make improvements in the quality of food in the dormitories.

_____

_____

10. The scientists conducted an <u>investigation</u> into the relationships within a large herd of giraffes in order to arrive at a determination of the strength of the bonds between female giraffes and their calves.

_____

_____

_____

Note: As you will see in the following exercise, using active voice often clarifies main ideas. Keep in mind, however, that passive voice has legitimate uses —in some scientific writing, for example, or when the writer wishes to shift emphasis from the performer of the action to the thing being acted upon. For additional practice in recognizing and using passive forms, see Exercises 21–3 and 21–4, pages 275–278.

7–5 Revising Sentences to Eliminate Passive Voice (*RHH,* 7g)

Underline passive verb forms in the following sentences. Then rewrite each sentence, making the verbs active. If you consider the passive form preferable in a particular sentence, put a check mark in the left margin, and be prepared to justify your choice. (In some cases—as in the example—you will need to supply a subject for the sentence.)

Example: During the three years of study in Africa, it <u>was observed</u> that wildebeests <u>were killed</u> by lions more often than any other prey.

During three years of study in Africa, one scientist observed that lions killed wildebeests more often than any other prey.

1. A pride of lions is formed by one or more family groups.

2. Cooperation is often used by pride members when they hunt.

3. Prey is sometimes chased by one lion toward another one waiting in ambush.

4. The lion—king of beasts—is often feared more than the tiger, but tigers are, in fact, larger and fiercer than lions.

139

5. It is often thought that lions kill freely and easily.

_____

_____

6. In fact, they often fail to catch their prey; on rare occasions they are even killed by the intended victim.

_____

_____

7. We know, for example, that a lion can be killed by blows from an adult giraffe's powerful legs.

_____

_____

8. When lions do manage to kill a giraffe, the carcass can be used as a source of food for several days.

_____

_____

9. Young giraffes rather than adults are killed most often.

_____

_____

10. Though it is a fairly rare occurrence, giraffes are sometimes pulled into rivers or pools and drowned by hungry crocodiles.

_____

_____

_____

7–6 Revising Sentences to Eliminate Delaying Formulas (*RHH,* 7h)

Revise the following sentences by eliminating delaying formulas, such as *it is, it was, there is, there was.* Make any other changes necessary to clarify main assertions.

Example: There were barely twenty years between the two world wars.

Barely twenty years elapsed between the two world wars.

1. It is usually the case that children learn to swim faster if they are taught early.

_____

_____

2. Some say that it is the television that is to blame for poor reading skills today.

_____

_____

3. It is argued by others that there has not been any serious decline in reading skills.

_____

_____

4. It is one of Barbara Tuchman's points in *A Distant Mirror* that there are striking similarities between the turmoil that has been characteristic of our century and the turmoil of the fourteenth century.

_____

_____

_____

5. In *The March of Folly* Tuchman suggests that there is reason to believe that governments often pursue policies that are contrary to their own interests, even when there are recognized and feasible alternatives to those policies.

_____

_____

_____

7–7 Review Exercise: Clarifying Main Ideas (*RHH,* 7a–h)

The following paragraphs contain sentences with unclear main ideas. Underline the key words in each paragraph—the ones that should carry the writer's meaning. Then revise for maximum clarity. Feel free to make any changes necessary to improve the paragraphs. Use your own paper.

PASSAGE 1

The failure of public school education is becoming a highly publicized issue in the media. Educators and politicians are concerned by the increasing evidence of low test scores and the number of unprepared high school graduates. This concern has led to federally and
5   locally funded studies of improvements that could be used to improve the system. One such study is being conducted in Austin, Texas, by the Select Committee on Public Education. Among the committee's many recommendations is a suggestion which Texans will find hard to accept. The Select Committee has determined that the extreme em-
10   phasis on athletics in the Texas public schools is part of the problem. Strong evidence has been presented in an attempt to convince the public that cutbacks in athletic programs are necessary.*

PASSAGE 2

As predicted, results in the present study show very clearly that a smile could make a person more likeable. Moreover, a smile literally increased one's face value. This positive evaluation effect is shown by the several attributes, apparently unrelated to smiling (be-
5   ing intelligent, good, bright, nice, pleasant), being ascribed to the smiling person. The fringe benefits of smiling seemed generous. The present study also found that the attraction effect of smiling tended to be more obvious on the male face.[20]

7–8 Review Exercise: Revising a Draft to Clarify Main Ideas (*RHH,* 7a–h)

Check the rough draft of your current essay for unclear main ideas. First, underline the main idea, and circle the subject and verb in each sentence. Then study the main idea in isolation, checking to see if you have aligned your meaning with grammatically important words, especially the subject and verb.

As you study the draft, look for other signs of unclear main ideas:

1. excessive use of the verb *to be* (is, are, was, were, has been, etc.)
2. unnecessary use of passive voice
3. unnecessary use of delaying formulas (it is, there is, there are, there were, etc.)
4. unnecessary use of *that* or *what* clauses

If your draft contains sentences with unclear main ideas, revise the sentences before submitting the final copy of your essay.

Note: As an alternative to the above exercise, you and a classmate may exchange drafts and check each other's work for unclear main ideas.

SUBORDINATION

7–9   Identifying Subordination (*RHH,* 7j)

Look in a book or magazine for a passage that contains subordination. Photocopy or write out the passage and underline the subordinate material. Be prepared to explain how the author uses subordination to achieve economy and to emphasize main ideas.

7–10   Identifying Subordination in Your Own Writing (*RHH,* 7j)

Photocopy or write out a page from one of your own essays. Underline the subordinate material, and be prepared to explain how the subordination helps to emphasize main assertions. Make note of any passage where your writing might be improved by further subordination. Use your own paper.

7–11   Combining Pairs of Sentences (*RHH,* 7j–m)

Combine each pair of sentences, turning one into a phrase or subordinate clause in the other.[21]

Example: Michael Hutchins and Victoria Stevens spent several years studying mountain goats in Olympic National Park. They hoped to help the National Park Service develop a plan for managing the animals.

In an effort to help the National Park Service develop a plan for managing its mountain goats, Michael Hutchins and Victoria Stevens spent several years studying the animals in Olympic National Park.

OR

Because Michael Hutchins and Victoria Stevens spent several years studying mountain goats in Olympic National Park, they may be able to help the National Park Service develop a plan for managing the animals.

1. Cougars, bobcats, coyotes, and golden eagles inhabit the Olympic Mountains. Hutchins and Stevens found little solid evidence that these animals prey on mountain goats.

   _____

   _____

   _____

   _____

2. An essential feature of the mountain goat's habitat is the alpine meadows. These meadows provide the animal's major food resource.

   _____

   _____

   _____

   _____

3. Mountain goats are like most animals inhabiting temperate regions. They must cope with seasonal fluctuations in food availability.

   _____

   _____

   _____

   _____

4. Food is abundant in the summer. Mountain goats then consume quantities in excess of their daily needs.

_____

_____

_____

5. Mountain goats have a craving for salt. Mineral licks are an important part of the mountain goat's ecology.

_____

_____

_____

6. National Park Service officials stopped providing salt for goats several years ago. They noticed that excessive trampling in the area of the salt lick was destroying plant life.

_____

_____

_____

7. Mountain goats are particularly susceptible to overheating. Their digestive system has a built-in furnace.

_____

_____

_____

8. Goats have colonies of microorganisms in their stomachs. These microorganisms generate heat as a result of their own metabolic processes.

_____

_____

_____

9. This heat is combined with the goat's own heat and with solar radiation. The excess heat can cause thermal stress.

_____

_____

_____

10. A mountain goat is often overheated and harassed by insects. It may lie in dirt and throw cool soil over its body with a foreleg.

_____

_____

_____

7–12 Using Free Subordinate Elements
(*RHH*, 7k–l)

Write ten sentences that contain free subordinate elements. Put brackets around the subordinate material. (Suggested topics for your sentences: politics, popular music, reading and writing, required college courses)

For sentences 1–6, use a free element at the beginning of the sentence to explain or place a condition on the main idea.

Example: [After the senator spoke with a group of her constituents,] she decided to vote for the farm bill.

1. _____

_____

_____

2. _____

_____

3. _____

_____

_____

4. _____

_____

_____

5. _____

_____

_____

6. _____

_____

_____

For sentences 7–8, use a free element at the end of the sentence to add a further thought.

Example: The president called the bill a boon for the economy, [a measure that would greatly increase farm production.]

7. _____

_____

_____

8. _____

_____

_____

For sentences 9–10, use a free element in the middle of the sentence to modify a particular word.

Example: Most farmers agreed that the bill, [a measure to lower interest rates], would greatly increase farm production.

9. _____

   _____

   _____

10. _____

   _____

   _____

7–13 Gaining Clarity through Free Subordination (*RHH,* 7k–l)

The following sentences are awkward because of excessive bound subordination. Underline the bound elements. Then rewrite each sentence, converting all or part of the underlined material into free subordinate elements. Make any other changes necessary to clarify the sentence.[22]

Example: An academic achievement test that was given to 600 sixth-graders from eight countries resulted in the finding that U.S. students scored last in mathematics, sixth in science, and fourth in geography.

In an academic achievement test given to 600 sixth-graders in eight countries, U.S. students scored last in mathematics, sixth in science, and fourth in geography.

1. More than a fifth of the students from one U.S. school that participated in the part of the test designed to determine whether students had a knowledge of geography could not locate the United States on a map of the world.

   _____

   _____

   _____

   _____

2. The warming of the Pacific Ocean called *El Niño* that spawned so much bad weather on the West Coast last winter also slowed the earth's rotation, according to meteorologists from Boston's Atmospheric and Environmental Research, Inc.

_____

_____

_____

_____

_____

3. The warm waters from *El Niño* created atmospheric pressures that were greater on the eastern side of mountain ranges and slowed the earth enough that the phenomenon created an extra one-fifth of a millisecond per day.

_____

_____

_____

_____

_____

4. Researchers at the University of Western Australia have invented a robot to shear sheep that has been used on hundreds of sheep during four years of testing while breaking the skin of the animals only a dozen or so times.

_____

_____

_____

_____

_____

5. The developers of the machine are working on a new model that may raise the amount of wool shorn per sheep from 70 to 95 percent that they hope will help fill the dwindling ranks of people who shear sheep.

_____

_____

_____

_____

_____

7–14 Revising to Eliminate Vague Subordination (*RHH,* 7m)

Rewrite the following sentences to eliminate vague subordination. Make any other changes necessary to clarify the sentences. (Your revisions need not contain free subordinate elements.)

Example: In terms of greatness, historians regard Abraham Lincoln as one of our greatest presidents.

Historians regard Abraham Lincoln as one of our greatest presidents.

1. With regard to Susan's request for a vacation in July, we decided to postpone it until August.

_____

_____

2. In the area of grades, I did very well last semester.

_____

_____

3. Seeing as how we were best friends ten years ago, why can't we get along now?

_____

_____

4. As far as math, I have nothing to worry about.

_____

_____

5. I don't think you and I are in full agreement in connection with your plan to spend the summer living rent-free at my parents' beach house.

_____

_____

7–15 Review Exercise: Using Subordination to Combine Sentences (*RHH*, 7j–m)

Combine each group of sentences into a single sentence, using at least one subordinate element, either bound or free. Experiment with several combinations until you find one that states the point clearly and concisely. Write your final version in the space provided.[23]

Example: The dandelion spreads rapidly. One year a single plant may grow in a field. A few years later the field may be covered with dandelions.

Because dandelions spread so rapidly, they may cover an entire field only a few years after a single plant has taken root there.

1. Dandelion leaves have jagged "teeth." The French called the plant *dent-de-lion*. This means "lion's tooth."

_____

_____

_____

2. The French name for the plant was adopted into the English language. *Dent-de-lion* came to be known as dandelion. The plant's scientific name is *Taraxacum officinale*.

_____

_____

_____

3. Dandelion stalks are hollow. A white, sticky sap oozes out from the cut end of this stalk. At one time scientists tried to make rubber out of this sap.

_____

_____

_____

4. Scientists had little success in making rubber. There is a Russian dandelion known as *kok-saghyz*. This plant does yield rubber.

_____

_____

_____

5. Dandelions have their uses. The fleshy root is a food for some people. They scrape the roots. Then they slice them. Then they boil them in salt water.

_____

_____

_____

6. The island of Minorca is east of Spain. The people there once stayed alive by eating dandelions. A swarm of locusts had destroyed all other green plants on the island.

_____

_____

_____

7. Dandelions are also used to make a beverage. The roots are cleaned. Then they are baked and ground. The result of this process is used as a coffee substitute or mixed with regular coffee.

_____

_____

_____

8. Many consider young dandelion leaves a tasty vegetable. The leaves of plants are gathered in early spring. They haven't flowered yet. The leaves are mixed with other greens in salads.

_____

_____

_____

9. The leaves of older plants are not used. They are too bitter. Seed houses have been developing new dandelion strains. These have larger leaves. The leaves taste better than wild dandelion leaves.

_____

_____

_____

10. Dandelion leaves can be cooked like spinach. When cooked, they lose some of their vitamin value. The leaves are rich in vitamins A and B. They also contain calcium, phosphorus, and iron.

_____

_____

_____

7–16 Review Exercise: Using Subordination in a Paragraph (*RHH,* 7j–m)

Combine the following sentences into a paragraph that contain several free subordinate elements. You may want to combine each numbered group of sentences into a single sentence, but you need not do so. There is no single correct answer; the example suggests one possible combination for the first group. Use your own paper.*

Example: When light came, I spotted two deer, a doe and a fawn.

1. Light came. I spotted two deer. One was a doe. The other was a fawn.

2. They highstepped through the grass. The grass was tall. They were in a clearing. They walked as if they were trying not to make a sound.

3. Suddenly they became frisky. Maybe the cold weather made them playful. Maybe it was the sun. It now shone through the tall grass. It seemed to raise their spirits.

4. Then something happened. The two deer vanished. Another one appeared. It was a magnificent buck.

5. The deer strutted. He was like a king. He came through an opening in the brush. He gradually moved closer.

6. My hands shook. I eased the gun up. I eased it up to my shoulder. I squeezed off a shot.

7. The shot broke the silence. The buck was startled. He crashed through the dense brush. He disappeared among the trees.

7–17 Review Exercise: Revising for Improved Subordination (*RHH*, 7j–m)

In a rough draft of your current essay, identify a paragraph that could be improved with further subordination. Revise the paragraph, using subordination to highlight main ideas and to make the writing as clear and forceful as possible. Submit the original paragraph along with your revision. Use your own paper.

Note: As an alternative to the above exercise, you and a classmate may exchange paragraphs (or complete drafts) and study each other's work to identify passages that could be improved with further subordination.

EMPHASIS

Note: The next three exercises will help you identify and use parallel elements to improve your writing. For additional practice in using parallelism, see Exercises 14–1, 14–2, and 14–3, pages 229–232.

7–18 Recognizing Matched Elements (*RHH*, 7n)

Underline matched elements in the following sentences. Then arrange the elements in groups to indicate parallel relationships, numbering each group as indicated in the example.[24]

Example: Let every nation know, whether it wishes us <u>well</u> or <u>ill</u>, that we shall <u>pay any price</u>, <u>bear any burden</u>, <u>meet any hardship</u>, <u>support any friend</u>, <u>oppose any foe</u> to assure the <u>survival</u> and the <u>success</u> of liberty.[24]

① well / ill ② pay any price / bear any burden / meet any hardship / support any friend / oppose any foe ③ survival / success

1. We observe today not a victory of party but a celebration of freedom, symbolizing an end as well as a beginning, signifying renewal as well as change.

_____

_____

_____

2. If a free society cannot help the many who are poor, it cannot save the few who are rich.

_____

_____

_____

3. Together let us explore the stars, conquer the deserts, eradicate disease, tap the ocean depths, and encourage the arts and commerce.

_____

_____

_____

4. Now the trumpet summons us again—not as a call to bear arms, though arms we need; not as a call to battle, though embattled we are; but a call to bear the burden of a long twilight struggle, year in and year out, "rejoicing in hope, patient in tribulation," a struggle against the common enemies of man: tyranny, poverty, disease, and war itself.

_____

_____

_____

_____

5. And so my fellow Americans, ask not what your country can do for you; ask what you can do for your country.

_____

_____

7–19 Using Anticipatory Patterns (*RHH,* 7o)

Write five sentences of your own using the anticipatory pattern indicated in parentheses. (Suggested topics for your sentences: teachers, clothing styles, holiday customs)

Example: (more *x* than *y*) *There is more reason to doubt his motives than to count on his financial support.*

1. (both *x* and *y*) _____

_____

_____

2. (either *x* or *y*) _____

_____

_____

3. (neither *x* nor *y*) _____

_____

_____

4. (not only *x* but also *y*) _____

_____

_____

5. (so *x* that *y*)_____

_____

_____

7–20 Using Series (*RHH*, 7q)

Use each of the following series in a sentence of your own. Make the series consistent and arrange it in a climactic order.

Example: (liberty, the pursuit of happiness, life)

In the Declaration of Independence, Thomas Jefferson specifically named three unalienable rights: life, liberty and the pursuit of happiness.

1. (discipline, hard work, persistence)

_____

_____

2. (the sciences, the social sciences, the humanities)

_____

_____

_____

3. (hot pink, blue, gray, black)

_____

_____

_____

4. (go home, get a good night's rest, take my medicine)

_____

_____

_____

5. (Phillip, Doris, their cat Pity Sing)

_____

_____

_____

7–21 Identifying Sentence Variety (*RHH,* 7r–w)

In the space provided, list several features that give variety to each paragraph.
One item is done for you as an example.

PASSAGE 1

For those who still argue about which came first, the chicken or
the egg, there is another philosophical question. Did the Finns
develop the sauna, or did the sauna develop the Finns? Did their
hardihood and endurance result from using these places of torture, as
5   they appear to the uninitiated, or did the Finns devise the sauna as a
testing ground because they already were that way? Nobody knows.
Since the sauna has been a part of Finnish culture for the past two
thousand years or more, it is an inseparable element in the formation
of the Finnish character.[25]

lines 2-3 – author uses a question

_____

_____

_____

_____

158

PASSAGE 2

Among the vices of age are avarice, untidiness, and vanity, which last takes the form of a craving to be loved or simply admired. Avarice is the worst of those three. Why do so many old persons, men and women alike, insist on hoarding money when they have no
5 prospect of using it and even when they have no heirs? They eat the cheapest food, buy no clothes, and live in a single room when they could afford better lodging. It may be that they regard money as a form of power; there is a comfort in watching it accumulate while other powers are dwindling away. How often we read of an old per-
10 son found dead in a hovel, on a mattress partly stuffed with bank-books and stock certificates! The bankbook syndrome, we call it in our family, which has never succumbed.[26]

7–22   Revising to Eliminate Choppiness (*RHH*, 7r–w)

The following passages consist largely of brief, plain statements with few internal pauses. Revise the passages, varying lengths and types of sentences and using subordination to highlight main ideas. Use your own paper.[27]

PASSAGE 1

What behavioral characteristics do many learning disabled students exhibit? Many learning disabled children have a short attention span. As a result, they have difficulty engaging in a single task for an entire period. They may become fidgety and inattentive. They may be easily distracted. In turn, they may distract others. The quality of their work may deteriorate. They may act out.

PASSAGE 2

Many learning disabled students have difficulty reading. The reading problems are varied. Some youngsters have poor decoding

159

skills. Some have poor comprehension. Some have difficulty read-ing handwritten materials. The textbooks for a course may be too difficult to read, though the content may be at a level understandable to the students.

7–23 Varying Sentence Length (*RHH,* 7r–w)

Write a very short sentence to follow each of the long sentences or passages given below. Be prepared to explain the effect you achieved by doing so.

Example: On their second try, after standing in the rain for over an hour, Casey and Karen finally approached the ticket window, confident that *this* time they would see the play.

They didn't.

1. After two weeks on vacation in Nova Scotia, Mr. Wiegand felt more relaxed than he had in years. But the long drive home had tired him, and as he pulled the car around the corner, he thought how wonderful it would be to sleep in his own bed again. As he came to a stop in the driveway, he shuddered at what he saw.

2. After lecturing for nearly two hours on inert gases, Professor Parks turned to the class, pointed to the blackboard, and smiled.

3. Many colleges and universities today claim that they have high admis-sions standards, that they offer strong preparation in the liberal arts, and that their graduates always find jobs.

4. The Fulmers watered their lawn every week, fertilized it three times during the summer, trimmed it, pampered it, all but talked to it. The next winter was mild, so in the spring they waited patiently for the first sprouts to appear.

5. Besides working full-time as a biologist, Jerry Farr served on the City Council, directed a local charity, and spent what little spare time he had doing volunteer work.

7–24 Finding Varied Sentence Patterns (*RHH*, 7t–w)

In a book, magazine, newspaper, or in the essay collection you use in your composition course, find a sentence that illustrates each of the following patterns. Copy the sentence on your own paper.

1. A sentence with an emphatic interruption
2. A sentence with inverted syntax
3. A cumulative sentence
4. A suspended sentence

7–25 Practicing Varied Sentence Patterns (*RHH*, 7t–w)

Write four sentences of your own, using as models the ones you found for the preceding exercise. Use your own paper.

8

Words

APPROPRIATE MEANING

8–1 Using a College Dictionary (*RHH*, 8a)

In order to become more familiar with the features of your college dictionary, use it to complete the following exercise.

Name of dictionary _____

A. ABBREVIATIONS AND LABELS

Where does your dictionary explain the abbreviations used in its entries?

_____

How does it abbreviate the following terms?

Example: adjective   *adj.*

1. noun   _____

2. conjunction   _____

3. verb   _____

4. plural   _____

5. transitive verb   _____

List five restrictive labels used in your dictionary.

Example: _slang_ _____

6. _____

7. _____

8. _____

9. _____

10. _____

B. PRONUNCIATION

List the pronunciations given by your dictionary for the following words.

Example: Augustine *ô'gə stēn'   ô gus'tin* _____

1. protein _____

2. literature _____

3. harass _____

4. Caribbean _____

5. hangar _____

6. often _____

7. poinsettia _____

8. miniature _____

9. mononucleosis_____

10. New Orleans _____

C. DERIVATION

Use the information given in your dictionary to explain the derivation of the following words.

Example: dandelion *Derived from Middle French, of dent de lion, literally tooth of (a) lion, translation of medieval Latin dens leonis, in allusion to the toothed leaves.*

1. daisy _____

   _____

   _____

2. bloomer (article of clothing) _____

   _____

   _____

3. astronaut _____

   _____

   _____

4. optic _____

   _____

   _____

5. biology _____

   _____

   _____

6. liberty _____

   _____

   _____

7. canine _____

_____

_____

8. Catholic _____

_____

_____

9. Jew _____

_____

_____

10. Protestant _____

_____

_____

D. SYNONYMS

Define the word *naive* and the synonyms that follow. Take care to distinguish each word from the others in the list.

1. naive _____

_____

_____

2. innocent _____

_____

_____

3. unsophisticated _____

_____

_____

4. unaffected _____

_____

_____

5. guileless _____

_____

_____

Use your dictionary to locate several synonyms for each of the following words.

Example: social _*amiable, companionable,*_
*genial, affable*

6. disaster _____

7. wind (noun) _____

8. sensuous _____

9. hide (verb) _____

10. talkative _____

8–2 Recognizing Connotation (*RHH,* 8d)

Circle the word in each pair that has a more favorable connotation—the suggested or implied meaning beyond its literal definition. Compare your answers with those of a classmate and discuss any differences. Be prepared to explain your choices.

Example: (childlike) / childish

1. slender / skinny

2. clever / sly

3. smell / odor

4. bachelor / spinster

5. nervous / high-strung

6. naughty / mischievous

7. recluse / hermit

8. timid / cowardly

9. guzzle / gulp

10. discerning / choosy

8–3 Changing Connotation within a Sentence (*RHH,* 8d)

Replace the italicized words in the following sentences with words that have more favorable connotations. Write your answer in the space provided.

Example: Nancy's performance on the test was *mediocre.* *average*

1. Ralph has *concocted* another theory about the missing documents. _____

2. Even as a baby, Becky was *finicky* about what she ate. _____

3. The dinner featured a *hodgepodge* of foods from the Middle East. _____

4. My uncle gave me a *lecture* on the evils of drinking. _____

5. I hadn't seen my grandmother in years; I was shocked by how *decrepit* she had become. _____

8–4 Selecting Words with Appropriate Connotations (*RHH,* 8d)

Circle the word in parentheses that carries the appropriate connotation for the context in which it appears. Be prepared to explain why you selected the word you did. Consult your dictionary as necessary.

Example: Lydia is the sort of ((person) / individual) everyone admires.

1. The baker (withdrew / removed) the hot loaves of bread from the oven.

2. The (scent / aroma) of freshly baked bread filled the room.

3. The (aroma / fragrance) of her perfume lingered in the car after she had gone.

4. Ken and Mary Grant were generous people, sharing their (opulence / wealth) with the entire Baraboo community.

5. We all admired the dignity and (pride / arrogance) with which Emma handled her fall from power.

6. In his notes, the biologist observed that the animal exhibited typical (catty / feline) behavior.

7. Dan had little (flair / aptitude) for decorating a room.

8. Despite his effort to make it cozy, the den still felt somewhat (cold / frigid).

9. The king was an imposing presence, (portly / stout) in body and lofty in carriage.

10. Although your paraphrase is generally accurate, it slightly (distorts / falsifies) what I said.

8–5 Using Connotation in a Paragraph (*RHH*, 8d)

Describe one of the following items twice, first creating a favorable impression, then an unfavorable impression. Use the same details in each passage, but select words whose connotations leave the reader with two distinct impressions. Use your own paper.

1. A plate of fried liver
2. A bouquet or corsage
3. A prom dress or tuxedo
4. An elderly person's hand
5. A wedding cake

8–6 Eliminating Sexist Language (*RHH*, 8e)

Edit the following sentences to eliminate sexist language and pronouns that needlessly suggest bias. Make your changes in the spaces above the lines.

Example: A dentist who fails the licensing exam on the first attempt may take it again in six months.

1. The university employs a staff of fifty cleaning ladies.

2. Each student is expected to finish his exam within two hours.

168

3. The NOW convention featured one session on women in the professions, which included speeches by several lady doctors.

4. According to the standard contract, the landlord or his agent will collect the rent on the first of each month.

5. Emily Dickinson is regarded today as an important poet. During her lifetime, however, Miss Dickinson published almost none of her work.

6. Even if a poet has published widely in periodicals, he will find it difficult to convince someone to publish his first book.

7. Until recently, a beginning grade school teacher in this state could expect her annual salary to be no more than $10,000.

8. The college hired several coeds to work at the bookstore during the first week of school.

9. The invention of movable type is one of man's greatest achievements.

10. As every housewife knows, the price of groceries has risen steadily in the past ten years.

8–7 Translating Jargon into Plain English
(*RHH*, 8f)

The following sentences mimic the wordy, pompous kind of jargon often used by government bureaucrats. Translate each sentence into the well-known saying hidden beneath the jargon.

Example: A period of pre-eminence is passed through by each and every canine.

Every dog will have its day.

1. Pulchritude does not penetrate the dermal plane.

   _____

2. It is fruitless to become lachrymal due to scattered lacteal material.

   _____

3. Articles which coruscate are not fashioned from aureate materials, at least not necessarily.

   _____

4. A feathered creature clasped in the manual members is the equivalent valuewise of a brace in the bosky growth.

   _____

5. Immature gallinaceons must not be calculated prior to their being produced.

   _____

8–8 Eliminating Jargon and Euphemisms (*RHH,* 8f–g)

Edit the following sentences to eliminate jargon and euphemisms. Make whatever changes are necessary to translate each passage into plain, straightforward English.

Example: The vice president asked the dean for feedback on a new plan to maximize the cost-effectiveness of the general education program.

The vice president asked the dean to comment on a new plan to make the general education program as economical as possible.

1. Because they are concerned about career needs, many students now select majors that will facilitate their attainment of technical skills.

   _____

   _____

   _____

170

2. Dan waited at the table while Denise went to the little girls' room to powder her nose.

_____

_____

3. Professor Wade asked her students to decide how the crisis in South America would impact election outcomes.

_____

_____

4. Lurline went to her reward yesterday. Tomorrow she will receive visitors at Kish-Burns Funeral Home, and on Friday she will be committed to her final resting place.

_____

_____

_____

5. Professor Frolick told us to take our time in completing the mid-term assessment instrument. He said he was in no hurry time-framewise.

_____

_____

_____

8–9 Revising a Passage to Eliminate Jargon (*RHH*, 8f)

Underline the jargon in the following passages. Then translate each passage into plain English, eliminating jargon, wordiness, overused expressions, and any other problems that cloud meaning. Use your own paper.

PASSAGE 1

The Department of Systems Management is seeking input from all personnel regarding the installation of an upgraded, cost-effective system of telephone-calling instruments in all corporate offices. The

171

department is prepared to up-front enough funding to upgrade the in-
5   struments that are operative at this point in time.

The decision-making process regarding upgrade-planning will proceed during the time frame of the next two months. At this point in time, personnel must initiate a determination of strategies that will maximize telephone usage efficiency. This office will (1) prioritize
10   those strategies, (2) determine how the strategies will impact the company, and (3) anticipate ways to facilitate the installation of new instruments.

PASSAGE 2

This project will attempt to determine the effect of classroom management strategies on the behaviors of learners at the third-grade elementary level. Group A will be managed by means of non-threatening feedback provided by the classroom teacher: the teacher
5   will ignore negative behaviors and will reward positive behaviors with positive oral feedback. Group B will be managed by punitive retention in the classroom during the recess period. At the end of ex-perimentation, an oral assessment will be obtained from classroom teachers in order to determine experimental outcomes. As a result of
10   the experiment, suggestions will be made to help teachers maximize the effectiveness of classroom management strategies.

8–10 Using Jargon for a Comic Effect
(*RHH,* 8f)

In the following piece of writing, a student retells Aesop's fable of the fox and the grapes, using jargon to achieve a comic effect. Study the piece, and be prepared to discuss how the writer's language changes the familiar story: what kind of writing is the student trying to parody? How does she do so? Then write your own version of a fable or fairy tale, trying for a similar effect. Use your own paper. Possible topics: the three little pigs, the tortoise and the hare, Goldilocks, Cinderella.

A Particular Fox and Some Grapes

One of the fox's desires is for ambulation, and in an excessively thermal, post-meridianic latitude one particular fox was exercising this quadruped means of self-transportation. While implementing this program of ambulation, he was awakened to the fact that the environment was abundantly populated by both herbaceous annual plants and temperate deciduous varieties.

A species of flora that came to immediate attention was the fruity byproducts of V. vinifera's propagatory instincts, lingering above as they always must. Upon spying these, the fox asked himself, "Would these fruits not satisfy my dehydrated condition?" And upon reaching an affirmative internal attitude, the fox adopted an upright posture and propelled himself upward in an effort to achieve his zenith. No luck, for gravity made nadir's approach much more efficient. Again and again he tried to resolve this classic approach-avoidance conflict exemplified by his desire for the fruity byproducts, but his inability to expend sufficient kinetic energy to propel himself within reach resulted in frustration and a violent decline to terra firma.

The conflict was, in essence, resolved when the fox postulated that he was either experiencing a visual hallucination, manifested in the form of grapes and induced by heat prostration and dehydration, or that in the event of their actual existence, said grapes were inclined to be immature and thus highly stimulatory to the bitterness sensors of the tongue surface. And besides, everyone knows that grapes are carcinogenic.*

LIVELINESS

8–11 Identifying Middle Diction (*RHH*, 8h)

Provide a middle diction equivalent for each slang or formal word in the following list. Consult your dictionary as necessary.

Examples: nefarious   *evil*

         stuck-up   *conceited*

173

1. nerd   _____

2. icky   _____

3. commence   _____

4. buddy   _____

5. cheapskate   _____

6. misprize   _____

7. pernicious   _____

8. pulchritude   _____

9. imbibe   _____

10. mix-up   _____

11. booze   _____

12. flagellate   _____

13. super (adjective)   _____

14. masticate   _____

15. hyper (adjective)   _____

8–12 Recognizing Formal Diction (*RHH*, 8h)

Underline the formal diction in the following passages, and be prepared to explain why the underlined words are appropriate for the context in which they appear. Note any other features that make the writing formal. Then rewrite one of the passages in a less formal style, relying mainly on middle diction. Use your own paper.

1. [Article III, Section 1, of the U.S. Constitution]

   The judicial Power of the United States, shall be vested in one supreme Court, and in such inferior courts as the Congress may from time to time ordain and establish. The Judges, both of the supreme and inferior Courts, shall hold their Offices during good behavior, and shall, at stated Times, receive for their Services, a Compensation, which shall not be diminished during their Continuance in Office.

2. [Abraham Lincoln speaking about the Civil War in his Second Inaugural Address]

Neither party expected for the war the magnitude or the duration which it has already attained. Neither anticipated that the cause of the conflict might cease with, or even before, the conflict itself should cease. Each looked for an easier triumph, and a result less fundamental and astounding.

3. [A formal invitation]

Mr. and Mrs. Alexander Bennington request the honor of your presence at the marriage of their daughter, Christina Lynne, to Mr. Gilbert Everett Fulmer, Saturday, the eighth of November, nineteen hundred and eighty-eight, at ten o'clock in the morning, St. David Church, 8500 Ridgeway, Great Neck, New York.

8–13 Recognizing Informal Diction (*RHH,* 8h)

Underline the informal diction or slang in the following passages, and be prepared to explain why the words are appropriate for the context in which they appear. Note any other features that make the writing informal. Then rewrite one of the passages in a more formal style, relying mainly on middle diction. Use your own paper.

1. [Huckleberry Finn, the young narrator of Mark Twain's novel, describing his life after the Widow Douglas adopts him]

At first I hated the school, but by-and-by I got so I could stand it. Whenever I got uncommon tired I played hookey, and the hiding I got the next day done me good and cheered me up. So the longer I went to school the easier it got to be. I was getting sort of used to the widow's ways, too, and they warn't so raspy on me. Living in a house, and sleeping in a bed, pulled on me pretty right, mostly, but before the weather was cold I used to slide out and sleep in the woods, sometimes, and so that was a rest to me. I liked the old ways best, but I was getting so I liked the new ones, too, a little bit.[28]

2. [American journalist Tom Wolfe describing whiskey runners]

   Whiskey running certainly had a crazy gamelike quality about it, considering that a boy might be sent up for two years or more if he were caught transporting. But these boys were just wild enough for that. There got to be a code about the chase. In Wilkes County nobody, neither the good old boys or the agents, ever did anything that was going to hurt the other side physically.[29]

3. [An informal invitation]

   Tom and I are planning a get-together this Friday night—nothing fancy, just a few folks from the neighborhood. Why don't you drop by for a drink and a bite to eat—around 8 or 8:30. Give us a call if you can't make it.

8–14 Revising to Eliminate Mixed Diction
(*RHH*, 8h)

The following passage contains an incongruous mixture of formal and informal language. Underline the offending words and replace them to make the passage consistent in its use of middle diction. Make your changes in the space above the lines. The first sentence is done for you as an example.

a woman
At the turn of the century, the female of the species was defined as someone's property. She was someone's mother, someone's daughter, or someone's wife—nothing more. She had few legal rights and therefore was stuck in her nowhere life. However, some members of the gender were experiencing an awakening. They were getting in touch with new feelings and were starting to envisage a future in which they might attain existence as people separate from their families.

In *The Awakening*, Kate Chopin delineates the life of such a woman—Edna Pontellier. Married to a rich New Orleans patrician, Edna discovers that her marriage is a big flop. Dimly cognizant of her own sensual and intellectual nature, she attempts to get it together as a person, seeking an independent life in which she defies social convention. Her happiness, however, is fleeting. Realizing that she is stuck with few alternatives, Edna chooses suicide rather than facing the conventional life from which she cannot extricate herself.

8–15 Revising to Eliminate Wordiness (*RHH*, 8i)

Revise the following passages to eliminate wordiness. Try several revisions on your own paper. Then copy the most concise version into the space provided. Watch for (1) redundancies, (2) circumlocutions, (3) excessive intensifiers, and (4) statements cast in negative form.

Example: Due to the fact that each and every person who came into the showroom would not have anything to do with the salesman, he did not sell a single, solitary car last weekend.

Because every customer in the showroom ignored him, the salesman sold no cars last weekend.

1. Maria said that the possibility exists that she might have the capacity to attend the party with a personal friend.

2. As far as the growing expansion of grain surpluses is concerned, it is quite likely that the Secretary of Agriculture might call upon the Congress to give its approval to the sale and exportation of grain to the Soviet Union.

3. In the area of books on scientific subjects, the public library is not without an ample supply of material.

    _____

    _____

4. Despite the fact that she is only two years of age, Bridget has the ability to do simple arithmetical problems that are more or less an impossibility for most children of her age.

    _____

    _____

    _____

5. It is not possible at the present time to make contact with the people who were witnesses at the time of the accident.

    _____

    _____

    _____

6. We circled around the incredibly steep mountain on a simply horrible road that was very narrow, but when we reached the very top of the mountain, the sensational view was certainly beautiful—not unlike some of the views I had seen in the Alps.

    _____

    _____

    _____

7. The press secretary said, "At this point in time, the president sees no reason to believe that there is cause for alarm in the matter concerning the placement by the Soviet Union of missiles in Cuba."

    _____

    _____

    _____

8. Each individual person at the seminar was asked to discuss his or her future plans and to explain what the end result of those plans would most likely be.

    _____

    _____

9. "First and foremost," said Casper, "I really do love your daughter Shirley, and I do so hope, Mr. Meuller, that you understand that I am desirous of asking you to make me the happiest man in the world by giving your blessing to the fact that your daughter and I wish to enter into the state of matrimony . . ." "Cease and desist," shouted Mr. Mueller. "Can't you manage to be less wordy and verbose?"

_____

_____

_____

_____

10. To make a long story short, eliminating excessive wordiness is quite simply a matter of careful revision. First, read and study your rough-draft prose in order to cut and excise verbose redundancies. Second, where circumlocutions are concerned, it is necessary that you find a somewhat shorter and more economical way to replace a needless phrase. Third, try to avoid the awful habit of adding an incredible number of perfectly useless intensifiers that just serve the quite unnecessary purpose of greatly fortifying and exaggerating simple statements that need no fortification or exaggeration. Finally, it is not a good idea to cast statements in a negative form unless it cannot be avoided; the negative form usually does not get the point across in a way that is as uncloudy as the positive form. Sometimes it is even not undifficult for the reader to grasp your meaning.

_____

_____

_____

_____

_____

_____

_____

_____

_____

8–16 Eliminating Wordiness in Your Own Writing (*RHH*, 8i)

Check the rough draft of your current essay and find five sentences that could be more concise. Revise them and submit your original sentences along with the revisions. Use your own paper.

8–17 Eliminating Clichés (*RHH*, 8j)

Revise the following passages to eliminate trite, overused expressions. Try several drafts on your own paper before copying the final version into the space provided. For many passages, you will need to supply new details and thoroughly rewrite the sentences in order to make the language fresh.

Example: My high school graduation is a day I shall never forget. I had the privilege of giving the valedictory address. Unfortunately, I had butterflies in my stomach, and during my speech I felt my heart in my throat. Right in the middle of the speech, I burst into a flood of tears.

Every time I'm asked to speak before a large group, I think about my high school graduation. I was so nervous about giving the valedictory address that I started crying halfway through the speech.

1. It has come to our attention that you are three months behind on your rent. It goes without saying that we expect your payment as soon as possible.

2. When my roommate complained bitterly about the grade on his history test, I told him that it was a dog-eat-dog world.

3. "And I'll be an old-fashioned Virginia housewife again," said Martha. "Steady as a clock, busy as a bee—and cheerful as a cricket."[30]

_____

_____

_____

4. Because of unforeseen circumstances in his negotiations with the Teamsters, the long suffering union boss was forced to announce that a strike was a foregone conclusion.

_____

_____

_____

5. In today's modern society, many people get trapped in a vicious circle of earning and spending money.

_____

_____

6. It goes without saying that a nuclear holocaust would pose a grave danger to humanity; we must do everything in our power to see that such a tragedy never occurs.

_____

_____

7. Claudia's flawless complexion beautifully complemented her sky-blue eyes and her silky brown hair.

_____

_____

8. Having sown his wild oats, Pat decided once and for all to settle down and devote himself fully to his career.

_____

_____

9. Mark and Joanne were head over heels in love, and we all waited with bated breath to see if they would set a date for their wedding. When we

could stand the suspense no longer, Mark explained that they would not be married in the near future because they simply didn't have enough money to make ends meet.

_____

_____

_____

_____

10. We heard a bloodcurdling scream in the bedroom. Mother said not to worry. It was just Dwight coming to terms with his feelings. He had been studying with a local primal scream therapist, learning how to handle aggression in a positive way.

_____

_____

_____

_____

8–18 Revising for Concreteness (*RHH,* 8k)

Make the language in the following paragraph more concrete, aiming for greater specificity and for fewer abstract words. Make any other changes necessary to improve the readability of the passage. The first sentence is done for you as an example. Use your own paper.

Example: (possible revision of the first sentence) *Divorce changes the way a child sees the family.*

> Divorce disrupts the child's perceptions of social reality. It confronts the child not only with loss but also with the need to reorder internal representations of familiar external patterns. Concepts of roles of father and mother and perceptions of the permanence of relationships must be revised. The rationale for the divorce is usually not clear to children of this age. The news of separation may come as a surprise even if the child knows that the parents are unhappy. Divorce is a cognitive puzzle for the child, bringing dissonance and inconsistency to the child's social and affective world. To deal with loss and to rearrange the disrupted perceptions demand time and energy that must be withdrawn from the work of the schoolroom and from social interaction with peers.[31]

8-19   Revising for Concreteness in Your Own Writing (*RHH,* 8k)

In a rough draft of your current essay, find a passage that could be improved by greater concreteness. Revise it and submit a copy of the original passage along with your revision. Use your own paper.

Note: The following exercise asks you to evaluate the effectiveness of figurative language. For practice in using figurative language in descriptive writing, see Exercises 1-7, 1-8, and 1-9, pages 7-11.

8-20   Evaluating Figurative Language (*RHH,* 8l)

Underline the figurative language in the following passages, and be prepared to explain why it is or is not effective.

1.   Clutter is the disease of American writing. We are a society strangling in unnecessary words, circular constructions, pompous frills and meaningless jargon.[32]

2.   Like all British police officers in Lower Burma, George Orwell lived in a pressure cooker.*

3.   Some lands are flat and grass-covered, and smile so evenly up at the sun that they seem forever youthful, untouched by man or time. Some are torn, ravaged and convulsed like the features of profane old age.[33]

4.   The humid air slapped my face like a hot wet blanket, and the burning air shot into my eyes like a knife.*

5.   When these students initiated the first sit-ins, their spirit spread like a raging fire across the nation, and the technique of non-violent direct action, constantly refined and honed into a sharp cutting tool, swiftly matured.[34]

IV

USAGE

9

Complete Sentences

9–1 Recognizing Subjects and Verbs (*RHH,* 9a)

Circle the main verb and underline the subject in each of the following sentences.[1]

Example: (a) <u>Beavers</u> (live) in colonies, one or more family groups to a lodge.

(b) A <u>family</u> usually (consists) of a mated pair and two sets of offspring.

1. Beavers are thickset animals with small, rounded ears, short legs, and large, webbed hindfeet.

2. Musk glands in both sexes produce a liquid used in perfumes.

3. The beaver's coat, consisting of a dense, fine underfur overlaid with many coarse guard hairs, is glossy tan to dark brown above, paler below.

4. The search for this fur stimulated some of the early 19th-century explorations of western North America.

5. Beavers show preference for streams and small rivers.

6. Their dams of sticks, stones, and mud may last for years, creating ponds that sometimes cover many acres.

7. Eventually, silt fills these ponds.

8. In rivers and lakes, beavers often burrow into banks.

9. Their food usually consists of the tender bark and buds of trees.

10. Branches, twigs, and small logs are anchored in the bottom mud in deep water for winter food.

9–2 Recognizing Independent Clauses (*RHH*, 9b)

Put brackets around the independent (or "main") clause in each of the following sentences. (Some sentences may have *two* independent clauses joined by a coordinating conjunction.)[2]

Example: (a) [Wool cloth was slightly easier to produce than linen.]

(b) After the sheep were sheared, [the fleece was picked through and brambles and other dirt removed.]

1. While some women by the late eighteenth century might have turned their skeins of thread over to a professional weaver, many still made their own cloth at home.

2. If the household was very large, a special weaving house might have been built to accommodate the loom.

3. The weaving itself consisted of pressing a foot treadle to separate the warp threads.

4. Since this work was done in spare moments between other chores, it might easily have taken a year for a wife to make her husband a cloth suit.

5. Such a garment was highly valued by its owner.

6. If producing a family's clothing might have been a pleasure, cleaning was never anything but drudgery.

7. Fortunately for the colonial woman, who already had great demands on her time, the standards of the eighteenth century were not high.

8. People washed their hands and faces, but they bathed only rarely.

9. Too much bathing was considered unhealthy—which it probably was when done in cold water in an unheated house during a New England winter.

10. Most people did not own many garments, and wash day came only once or twice a year.

9–3 Recognizing Subjects, Verbs, and Independent Clauses in Your Own Writing (*RHH*, 9a–b)

Photocopy or write out a page from one of your own essays. Circle the main verb and underline the subject in each sentence. Then put brackets around each independent clause.

9–4 Sentence Practice: Joining Fragments and Independent Clauses (*RHH*, 9b–c)

The following items are fragments—dependent clauses treated as complete sentences. In the space provided, connect each fragment to an independent clause to form a complete sentence.

Example: As soon as she finished the history exam.

As soon as she finished the history exam, Susan began to study for her math quiz.

OR

Betty said that she would talk to Sam as soon as she finished the history exam.

1. After the party was over.

_____

_____

_____

2. Because he was bald and overweight.

_____

_____

_____

3. Before his tax refund arrived.

_____

_____

_____

4. Although many women now work outside the home.

_____

_____

_____

5. If you hope to succeed in college.

_____

_____

_____

9–5 Eliminating Sentence Fragments (*RHH,* 9b–c)

Eliminate the fragments in each of the following passages by combining the elements into a single sentence or by rewriting fragments as independent clauses.

Example: Most banks now offer high-interest certificates of deposit. Along with passbook savings accounts.

Along with passbook savings accounts, most banks now offer high-interest certificates of deposit.

1. Asian and African elephants differ in size. The African elephant being larger.

_____

_____

_____

2. The albatross, like most sea birds, lays only one egg a year. Both parents helping to care for the single chick when it hatches in February or March.

_____

_____

_____

3. Mars has two satellites, Phobos and Deimos. Which are both closer to Mars than the moon is to the earth.

_____

_____

_____

4. Many types of fruit thrive in the Yakima Valley. Such as apples, peaches, apricots, and cherries.

_____

_____

_____

5. Many are leaving the teaching profession today. Partly as a result of low salaries and poor working conditions.

_____

_____

_____

9–6 Editing a Passage to Eliminate Sentence Fragments (*RHH,* 9b–c)

Edit the following passages to eliminate sentence fragments. Make the necessary changes by underlining each fragment and writing your revisions in the space above the lines. Two fragments are corrected as examples.

PASSAGE 1

Scientists have recently discovered 6,000,000-year-old ice on a glacier in Antarctica. ~~By~~ *It is by* far the oldest ice ever found.

New ice near the surface of the glacier is evaporating~~/~~, ~~E~~*e*xposing layer upon layer of ancient ice that contains volcanic dust, carbon
5   dioxide and other materials that have accumulated over the years. Usually, such complete records are obtained only by drilling deep ice cores. Such as the 6,500-foot-long vertical shaft that researchers obtained in Greenland last year. The stratified layer of that core providing a continuous climatic history of the world for the past 125,000
10   years. The oldest such information now on record.

The Antarctic glacier is littered with hundreds of meteorites. Some of which are 7,500,000 years old. From these remnants, Ian Whillans of Ohio State University and other scientists were able to establish the age of the ice.[3]

PASSAGE 2

Americans are now using 450 billion gallons of water a day. According to a recent report from the U.S. Geological Survey. The figures represent a 200-percent increase in water use over the past 30 years, but the survey says daily use falls far short of the 1,200 billion
5   gallons the country can supply every day. Not including extensive groundwater resources.

The figures, which cover the 1975–1980 period, include water used for all purposes. Public supply, industry, irrigation, rural and commercial. Industry makes the biggest drain on the water supply—
10   260 billion gallons a day. Eighty-three percent of which goes to thermoelectric power. Idaho uses more water than any other state. Rhode Island using the least water.[4]

9–7 Recognizing Intentional Fragments (*RHH*, 9d)

Copywriters often use fragments intentionally when writing copy for magazine advertisements. Underline each fragment in the following copy. Why did the writer use fragments instead of complete sentences? On your own paper, rewrite the passage in a more formal style by eliminating all fragments. How does your "translation" affect the copy?[5]

A copier is one of those things that people notice when it's not working.

Which is why an IBM Model 60 Copier tends to become invisible.

It's so reliable, people take it for granted.

A computer inside helps keep it running smoothly. So you get consistently high quality copies. And many easy-to-use features.

Like automatic duplexing. A semi-automatic feed. And a job-interrupt feature, which can allow small jobs to interrupt big ones.

9–8 Sentence Practice: Joining Independent Clauses (*RHH*, 9e)

Write ten sentences, using two independent clauses in each. In the first five, join the clauses with a comma and the coordinating conjunction given in parentheses. In the remaining five, use a semicolon. (Suggested topics for your sentences: sports, dangerous occupations, politicians)

Example: (but) *A 1967 study listed astronauts as the worst insurance risk, but race car drivers were not far behind.*
(semicolon) *Richard Nixon took office on January 20, 1969; he resigned on August 9, 1974.*

1. (and) _____

_____

_____

2. (but) _____

_____

_____

3. (for) _____

_____

_____

4. (so) _____

_____

_____

5. (yet) _____

_____

_____

6. _____

_____

_____

7. _____

_____

_____

8. _____

_____

_____

9. _____

_____

_____

10. _____

_____

_____

9-9 Sentence Practice: Joining Independent Clauses with Sentence Adverbs and Transitional Expressions (*RHH*, 9e)

Write five sentences of your own, each containing two independent clauses joined by a semicolon and the word or phrase given in parentheses. (Suggested topics for your sentences: women and careers, television, current events)

Example: (therefore) *Nina does the same work as Patrick; therefore she should receive the same salary.*

1. (however) _____

_____

_____

2. (furthermore) _____

_____

_____

3. (thus) _____

_____

_____

4. (for example) _____

_____

_____

5. (on the other hand) _____

_____

_____

9-10 Identifying and Eliminating Run-On Sentences (*RHH*, 9e)

In the space provided, indicate whether each sentence is correct (C) or is a run-on sentence (RO). Then eliminate the errors, using one of the two methods illustrated in the examples. Make the necessary changes in the space above the lines. (Watch for sentence adverbs or transitional phrases that may disguise run-on sentences.)[6]

Example: (comma and coordinating conjunction)

, but

Pigs are herd animals we seldom notice it because

we keep the animals confined.   *RO*

(semicolon)

;

Pigs are like other flocking or herding animals/

they follow that system of bosses and underlings

known as "pecking order."   *RO*

1. A senior boar will lead the herd, when there is no boar loose with the sows, an older and experienced sow rules the sty.   _____

2. Pigs can be as absolutely brutal to one of their number as can a bunch of chickens bent on pecking a sickly pullet to death.   _____

3. Pigs are famous for wallowing they wallow by choice when the weather is hot.   _____

4. They wallow both to cool themselves and to help thwart external parasites.   _____

5. Tanned pigskin is tough, however, the skin while on the pig is hardly more resistant to scratches or bites than our own.   _____

6. Slap a white pig, your hand leaves a red welt.   _____

7. Fly and mosquito bites leave the red spots and blotches characteristic of a bad case of the measles.   _____

196

8. Pigs are not well equipped to cope with either high or low temperatures, in fact, piglets are totally incapable of regulating their body temperatures for the first two or three days after birth.   _____

9. Adult pigs have few sweat glands, and most of those are on their snouts.   _____

10. When the weather is hot, they must seek a cool spot in which to lie, they seek shade and/or a wallow.   _____

9–11 Eliminating Comma Splices (*RHH,* 9e)

Eliminate the comma splices in the following sentences, using one of the three basic methods illustrated in the example. Use each method at least twice. Make the necessary changes in the space above the lines.*

Example: (separate sentences)

The largest city in Vietnam was once called Saigon, it is known today as Ho Chi Minh City.

(comma and coordinating conjunction)

The largest city in Vietnam was once called Saigon, it is known today as Ho Chi Minh City.

(semicolon)

The largest city in Vietnam was once called Saigon, it is known today as Ho Chi Minh City.

1. Writing is much like any other skill, it improves with practice.

2. I find that writing a rough first draft is very difficult, I like to revise as I write.

3. In writing a draft, I try to avoid all errors, this prevents me from concentrating on the idea I am trying to develop.

4. My ability to organize my essays has improved during the semester, furthermore, I now develop my ideas more fully and give enough detail to make each point convincing.

5. I try to cover too many ideas in my papers, in doing so, I don't do an adequate job with any of them.

6. My high school placed too much emphasis on athletics, it gave little credit to those interested in school work.

7. During my junior year, classes were easy, they were also crowded because the money allotted for more classrooms was mysteriously spent on a new band hall.

8. The school's air conditioners broke down every few weeks, this left students to bake in the South Texas heat.

9. The classrooms needed paint, the potholes in the parking lot swallowed cars.

10. I decided to sign up for the school's highly respected vocational education program, however, upon inspecting my record, the director of the vocational department refused to admit me because my grades were too high.

Note: Exercise 9–11 illustrates three basic methods for eliminating comma splices. The following exercise introduces another method that is often useful in bringing out logical relationships within a sentence—subordinating one element to another. For further practice in using subordination, see Exercises 7–9 through 7–17, pages 143–154.

9–12 Using Subordination to Eliminate Comma Splices (*RHH,* 9e)

Eliminate the comma splices in the following sentences by converting one element of each sentence into a phrase or a subordinate clause. Write your revisions in the space provided. (You might want to compare the revised sentences for this exercise with those for Exercise 9–11, noting how the various methods of eliminating comma splices affect meaning.)

Example: The largest city in Vietnam was once called Saigon, it is known today as Ho Chi Minh City.

(phrase) *Once called Saigon, the largest city in Vietnam is known today as Ho Chi Minh City.*

(subordinating clause) *Although it is known today as Ho Chi Minh City, the largest city in Vietnam was once called Saigon.*

1. Writing is much like any other skill, it improves with practice.

_____

_____

_____

2. I find that writing a rough first draft is very difficult, I like to revise as I write.

_____

_____

_____

3. I try to cover too many ideas in my papers, in doing so, I don't do an adequate job with any of them.

_____

_____

_____

4. My high school placed too much emphasis on athletics, it gave little credit to those interested in schoolwork.

_____

_____

_____

5. The school's air conditioners broke down every few weeks, this left
   students to bake in the South Texas heat.

9-13 Editing a Passage to Eliminate Run-On Sentences (*RHH,* 9e)

Edit the following passage to eliminate fused sentences and comma splices.
Make the necessary changes in the space above the lines. The first error is
corrected for you as an example.[7]

The Vikings had many reasons for their reckless pursuits; it
would seem that they engaged in dangerous ventures to prove themselves valiant and courageous. Upon returning from one of their
many fierce voyages, they were warmly welcomed by their native

5 people, who celebrated their return with exuberance, usually for
days at a time. Women served horns filled with mead amid drinking
and laughter the Vikings would play games of chance, using dice and
counters. Sometimes they sent up burnt offerings to the gods, they
always sang of their forefathers' achievements, lustily drinking to

10 even greater deeds in days to come.

Every hardy Norseman was expected to engage in war, the cus-
tomary weapons were battle-ax, sword, and bow. Wearing a conical
helment with nose cover and a coat of mail or leather garment, the
warrior felt well protected, however, at times he would show his

15 courageous nature by removing his shirt (*serk*) before a battle. Armed
only with a club, he would engage his enemy in combat, the term
berserk, meaning "without a shirt," stems from this demonstration.

200

10

Subject–Verb Relations

10–1 Eliminating Mixed Constructions (*RHH*, 10a)

Edit the following sentences to eliminate mixed constructions. Make the necessary changes in the space above the lines.

Example: Even though my nine brothers and sisters are scattered across
 *we meet every year*
Canada, ~~is not enough to stop our annual meeting~~ in Toronto.

1. When designing a house was the best part of the architecture course I took last fall.

2. His uncle gave it to him the beagle he had seen in the pet shop.

3. The first-time homebuyer, he should hire a professional inspector to evaluate the condition of any house he plans to buy.

4. Whenever the four of them got together was the time they talked for hours about their college days.

5. Marcia told Bill that when he came for dinner on Tuesday would be ample time to discuss his bid for a seat on the council.

6. The audience, they roared in approval when the band members leapt onto the stage.

7. Dr. Torok, her husband, and their family, they were honored for long and tireless service to the community.

8. Alfred Sullivan won it for singing "The Wearing of the Green" the award for best solo at the Bay City Songfest.

9. What you see it is what you get.

10. When in doubt is the time to punt.

10-2 Matching Subjects with Verbs
(RHH, 10b)

Circle the verb in parentheses that agrees with the subject.

Example: dolphins (is valued, (are valued))

1. a whale (lives, live)

2. whales (swims, swim)

3. there (is, are) whales

4. whales of this type (survives, survive)

5. school of whales (consists, consist)

6. whale and dolphin (is hunted, are hunted)

7. neither a whale nor a dolphin (has been found, have been found)

8. every whale and dolphin (survives, survive)

9. Flipper, along with many other dolphins, (performs, perform)

10. *Moby-Dick,* a book about whales, (is read, are read)

10–3 Subjects and Verbs:
Singular to Plural (*RHH*, 10b)

Rewrite each of the following sentences, making the subjects and verbs plural. Circle the words you change.

Example: The (potato)(is) high in fiber.

Potatoes are high in fiber.

1. The potato was first cultivated in South America nearly 2,000 years ago.

2. Today, it is a major world food staple.

3. The tomato also comes from South America.

4. When first introduced in Europe, it was thought to be poisonous.

5. Today, the tomato is an important food source in southern Europe, especially Italy.

10–4 Identifying Subject–Verb Agreement
(*RHH*, 10b)

Underline the subject and circle the correct verb form in each of the following sentences. In the space provided, indicate whether the verb you circle is singular (S) or plural (P).[8]

Example: The <u>absence</u> of trees ((makes) make) the Arctic

landscape appear lifeless, bare, and desolate.   *S*

1. But there (is, are) unexpected richness of life. _____

2. Lichens, mosses, grasses, and flowering plants (forms, form) a continuous cover over the thin humus layer. _____

3. But the mammals (is, are) most impressive, from the little Arctic mouse to polar bears, caribou, and musk oxen and lemmings. _____

4. And there (a) (is, are) innumerable birds, many of which (b) (remains, remain) in the Arctic only during the summer. (a) _____ (b) _____

5. Whether plant or animal, every living organism (has adapted, have adapted) in its own way to the extreme environment. _____

6. As everywhere, the soils of the Arctic (represents, represent) the basis of all life on land. _____

7. High Arctic desert soils commonly (displays, display) ephemeral salt crusts. _____

8. The chemical reaction of these soils (is, are) usually neutral to alkaline. _____

9. The low soil temperatures, even in summer (a) (means, mean) that nitrogen-producing bacteria (b) (breaks, break) down the organic material extremely slowly. (a) _____ (b) _____

10. Where bird droppings or animal carcasses (a) (fertilizes, fertilize) the soil, a remarkably luxuriant vegetation soon (b) (flourishes, flourish). (a) _____ (b) _____

204

10–5 Eliminating Errors in Subject–Verb Agreement (1) (*RHH,* 10b–e)

In the following sentences, circle any verbs that do not agree with their subjects. Then write the correct verb form in the space provided. Write C in the space if there is no error.[9]

Example: Most stars in the universe ⟨has⟩ masses of one-

tenth to fifty times the mass of our sun.   *have*

1. Just a few light-years from our solar system lie a cold, dark, invisible object. _____

2. Only a twentieth of the sun's mass, it still retain the small planetary system that was born with it. _____

3. But these planets whirl about their sun in darkness, for the star does not shine. _____

4. Any light that touches their chill surfaces come from other stars. _____

5. This dark star are neither a black hole nor a neutron star. _____

6. It is a black dwarf—a star so small its core never grew hot enough to ignite. _____

7. Stars of all kinds are born in dusty gas clouds like the Orion and Lagoon Nebulae. _____

8. Some of these has many times the sun's mass, while others are smaller. _____

9. The nebula's temperature and density determines how large or small a given star will turn out to be. _____

10. The laws of physics shows that a star below a certain critical mass will never become hot enough to initiate thermonuclear fusion of hydrogen in its core. _____

10–6 Eliminating Errors in Subject–Verb Agreement (2) (*RHH*, 10b–e)

The following sentences contain the type of subject-verb agreement errors that writers often overlook in revising first drafts. Review the rules for agreement; then carefully locate and circle each incorrect verb form. Write the correct form in the space provided.

Example: Each of the winners (were) honored at a reception following the competition.   *was*

1. The number of degrees granted by American colleges and universities have increased steadily over the past twenty years.   _____

2. Unfortunately, the college graduate who enter the job market today may well be underemployed.   _____

3. There is more and more stories about cab drivers who display their diplomas on the dashboards of their cabs.   _____

4. Even having three diplomas—a B.A., an M.A., and a Ph.D.—do not guarantee a job, as many unemployed college professors will testify.   _____

5. Despite the surplus of graduates, the number of new students are still growing every year at some colleges.   _____

6. At some universities, a virtual army of freshmen enlist in computer courses, hoping to enter a new and lucrative job market.   _____

7. English and history, once popular fields of study, now gives way to more "practical" disciplines.   _____

8. Neither art nor music are required in many college
    curriculums today.   _____

9. What is the likely results of the current trend
    toward narrow technical training?   _____

10. Some complain that intense specialization, along
    with a lack of preparation before college, too often
    result in graduates without basic skills in reading,
    writing, and thinking.   _____

10–7 Editing a Passage to Eliminate Errors in Subject–Verb Agreement (*RHH,* 10b–e)

Edit the following passages, correcting errors in subject-verb agreement. Make the necessary changes in the space above the lines. One error is corrected as an example.[10]

PASSAGE 1

According to the World Health Organization in Geneva, physicians m̶a̶k̶e̶s *make* up a relatively small proportion of the community at
large. In none of the countries listed are there more than one doctor
per 200 people. Clearly, an abundance of doctors are a good thing, but
5   it do not necessarily follow that the general health of the inhabitants of
a country improve as doctors become more plentiful. For example,
the Soviet Union, with the highest proportion of physicians among the
countries listed, are currently beset by serious health problems, a high
infant-mortality rate, and a declining life expectancy.

PASSAGE 2

Using a genetically engineered form of interferon administered
by nasal-spray dispensers, a group of British and French scientists
have proved that the substance is effective in blocking a common-

cold virus. Previous studies has shown that the much more expen-

5 sive form of interferon, which is derived from human cells, also
work against colds, but this is the first time that interferon cloned
from bacteria have been tested.

10–8 Review Exercise: Fragments, Run-on Sentences, and Subject–Verb Agreement (*RHH*, 9, 10)

Edit the following draft, correcting fragments, comma splices, fused sentences, and errors in subject-verb agreement. Make the necessary changes in the space above the lines.*

He thunder across the glossy pages of every popular magazine. He and his trusty steed alone in the wilderness, at one with nature, a symbol of everything masculine, a man in the purest sense of the word. He is the Marlboro Man who, along with his cohorts the Camel Man and the Chaz Guy, have become a symbol of the American male. An image for all men to emulate.

Newspapers, magazines, and television spends millions of dollars each year selling this image to the public, thus they shapes the way we view ourselves. Giving us a highly inaccurate picture of what it means to be "masculine." The media man is cool, aloof, and rugged he is so secure in his own maleness that female companionship, tenderness, and sensitivity is seldom, if ever, a part of his image.

We've all seen the infamous Old Spice Man. Making his glorious return from the sea. After ten months aboard ship, he seem cool and assured when welcomed by his waiting girl, she kept herself busy by knitting her man a sweater. After all, why should she entertain thoughts of an affair, her man uses Old Spice.

11

Modifiers

11–1 Recognizing Modifiers:
Words, Phrases, and Clauses (*RHH,* 11a)

In each group of sentences, underline the type of modifier indicated.

Examples: Words
He <u>often</u> gave <u>his</u> wife red roses or boxes of <u>rich</u> <u>chocolate</u> candies.

Phrases
At <u>the last minute</u>, Judy changed her plans <u>for the Christmas party</u>.

Subordinate clauses
The girl <u>who was dressed as a bunch of grapes</u> won the prize for the most original costume.

SENTENCES 1–4: WORDS

1. Sometimes the best way to impress people is to remain absolutely silent.

2. The brightest room in the house was Dorothy's, a big, second-floor study with six windows and a high ceiling.

3. Unfortunately, the police acted too quickly and arrested the wrong man.

4. She opposed capital punishment because of its often unfair and erratic application.

SENTENCES 5–7: PHRASES

5. In some elections, the candidate with charm defeats the one with ideas.

6. The cook sighed, looking with pride at the dozen pumpkin pies lining the shelf.

7. Unable to resist any longer, Amanda took out her wallet and bought the coat with her rent money.

SENTENTENCES 8–10: SUBORDINATE CLAUSES

8. When they added up the time they had spent playing Trivial Pursuit, they decided to throw the game away.

9. Most scientists believe that Pluto, which was discovered in 1930, is the outermost planet in our solar system.

10. Although he is short and small-framed, Pablo is a good athlete.

11–2 Recognizing Modifiers in a Passage
(*RHH*, 11a)

Place brackets around one clause, underline four phrases, and circle five words that function as modifiers in the following passage. (Notice that one modifying element may appear *within* another—as in the examples that are marked for you.)[11]

It is not hard to identify the source of our fear of sharks—the idea of being eaten alive is obviously what makes people so afraid. The white shark has acquired a reputation for mindless ferocity that is probably unequaled among terrestrial or aquatic predators. But along with our fear there is an admiration, a morbid fascination with this sleek, powerful, menacing monster [that can be found in practically all the (temperate) oceans <u>of the world</u>.]

11-3 Sentence Combining: Placing Modifiers (*RHH*, 11b)

Combine the following pairs of sentences, using the underlined part of the second sentence as a modifier in the first. There are no single "correct" answers for this exercise. Work with each pair until you devise a combination that seems clear and effective. Write your final version in the space provided, punctuating as necessary.

Example: Beethoven conducted the first performance of his Ninth Symphony in 1823. He was <u>totally deaf at the time</u>.

Although he was totally deaf at the time, Beethoven conducted the first performance of his Ninth Symphony in 1823.
OR/
Beethoven, totally deaf at the time, conducted the first performance of his Ninth Symphony in 1823.

1. Thomas Jefferson and John Adams died on July 4, 1826. This day was <u>the fiftieth anniversary of American Independence</u>.

_____

_____

_____

2. Coffee is regarded by some today as a potentially harmful stimulant. Coffee was <u>once used in Arabia as a medicine</u>.

_____

_____

_____

3. *The Sun*, a British newspaper, commemorated Queen Victoria's coronation in 1838. The newspaper did so by <u>printing an entire issue in gold ink</u>.

_____

_____

_____

5. _____

_____

_____

11–6 Eliminating Dangling Modifiers (*RHH*, 11c)

Underline the dangling and misplaced modifiers in the following sentences. Then revise each sentence, relating modifiers clearly and effectively to the words they modify. If a sentence contains no problems with modification, write C in the space provided.*

Example: The company says that there is little evidence to link "second-hand smoke" with disease in nonsmokers <u>in its advertisement</u>.

In its advertisement, the company says that there is little evidence to link "second-hand smoke" with disease in nonsmokers.

But <u>when smoking in public places</u>, greater consideration is needed.

But when smoking in public places, smokers should show greater consideration.

1. Like the other advertisement, the reader will find this one puzzling.

_____

_____

_____

2. After comparing the three ads, the one with muted colors had the greatest effect.

_____

_____

_____

3. The advertisement only was found in two of the five magazines we surveyed.

_____

_____

_____

4. To gain the reader's attention, magazine advertisers use every conceivable tactic, legal or otherwise.

_____

_____

_____

5. Once placed in a magazine, readers will stop and read this advertisement.

_____

_____

_____

6. Some advertising aimed at the elderly primarily appeals to a fear of financial insecurity.

_____

_____

_____

7. The black background of the page may be the key to the advertisement's success; being black, the bright orange letters stand out.

_____

_____

_____

8. Lewis Thomas, a medical doctor, writes movingly in his essay, "The Long Habit," about death.

   _____

   _____

   _____

9. Offering scientific information about the nature of dying, anecdotes are used as well.

   _____

   _____

   _____

10. By using a personal tone to relate scientific information, our fear of death is placed in a new light.

    _____

    _____

    _____

11. Thomas claims that he has seen agony in death only one time.

    _____

    _____

12. One of the most important functions of the doctor was to provide comfort at the moment of death in the past.

    _____

    _____

    _____

13. Citing a nineteenth-century source about a man crushed in the jaws of a lion, Thomas suggests that the moment of death may not be as terrifying as we imagine it to be.

_____

_____

_____

_____

14. Some scientists theorize that all creatures are equipped with a physiological mechanism that takes effect and induces tranquillity when dying.

_____

_____

_____

_____

15. In concluding his essay about death, a humorous touch is used.

_____

_____

_____

11–7   Punctuating Modifiers (*RHH,* 11h–p)

In the following sentences, underline any modifying words, phrases, or clauses that require punctuation. Then add commas where necessary, circling each one as shown in the example. Circle the number of any sentence that requires no additional commas.[12]

Example: Huge aggregations of garter snakes‿at times numbering 10,000 to 15,000‿have drawn the attention of herpetologists to the Interlake region of southern Manitoba.

1. Since the snakes cannot withstand freezing temperatures they must hibernate during the winter.

2. The study of the red-sided garter snake which ranges the farthest north of any snake in North America sheds light on how reptiles have adapted to cold environments.

3. The garter snakes emerge from hibernation in late April or early May.

4. First large numbers of males appear.

5. Soon after females leave the communal den emerging singly or in small groups over a period of several weeks.

6. The mass emergence of male snakes as opposed to the delayed staggered emergence of females may have adaptive value.

7. With the ratio of males to females as high as 50 to 1 the probability of females being fertilized is virtually 100 percent.

8. Also if females were to emerge together, mate, and disperse early in the season unpredictable freezing temperatures might destroy much of the breeding population.

9. The staggered return to activity of the females ensures that some will survive.

10. As soon as they have mated females leave the den site and disperse to summer feeding areas.

11. Consequently the total time they are exposed to predators at the den site is reduced.

12. The bulk of the population that remains around the den for any length of time is male—and somewhat more expendable.

13. As soon as a female appears on the surface she is mobbed by male suitors.

14. The male's vigorous courtship behavior is triggered by the sudden change in body temperature coincident with emergence from the den.

15. In the laboratory male red-sided garter snakes court females within ten minutes after a transfer from a cold dark environment to a warm lighted one.

16. This sequence simulates the normal transition from hibernation to immediate posthibernation conditions.

17. When they are kept cold and merely transferred from darkness to light male garter snakes fail to exhibit courtship behavior.

18. The change in body temperature irrespective of light conditions appears to be the principal factor in triggering mating behavior.

19. Male courtship behavior lasts for three to four weeks waning over time.

20. Surprisingly enough the snakes do not eat during the mating period.

11–8 Review Exercise: Placing and Punctuating Modifiers (*RHH*, 11b–p)

Edit the following draft for errors in the placement and punctuation of modifiers. Make the necessary changes in the space above the lines. You may want to copy your revised version onto a separate sheet of paper before submitting it. One sentence is revised for you as an example.*

Although changed by several drastic remodeling projects over
the years, I always, feel comfortable. in our home on Belvin Street.
our home on Belvin Street always makes me
My family has many good memories of the house, even though
we've only owned it for eleven years. Affectionately called "the old

5   stack of boards" by my father, my mother who is more sentimental
than he is speaks of its warmth and security fondly.

Built around 1900 by modern standards the foundation of the
house is inadequate; the structure rests on piers made of huge old
cedar stumps not of concrete. Extending out to four full-length col-

10   umns, at one time there was a balcony. It was removed long ago
judged structurally unsound.

15   Five large bedrooms but one bath only are upstairs. Downstairs the living room is in the front part of the house. A large elegant room, it has a fireplace in the middle of a varnished wooden wall which is made of red bricks. Behind the living room just beyond a hand-carved wooden door is the dining room. From here one can see the modern kitchen a room that still retains a hint of its turn-of-the-century charm. Finally used in the past as a parlor or library on the other side of the kitchen is a small office.

12

Cases of Nouns and Pronouns

12–1 Identifying Correct Pronoun Cases (*RHH,* 12a–i)

Review the various rules governing case; then circle the correct pronouns within the parentheses in the following exercise.

Example: My roommate and ((I)/ me) had an argument last week about

((who) / whom) would control the volume of the stereo.

1. He argued that if the stereo doesn't disturb (his / him) studying, then it

    shouldn't disturb the studying of the student (who / whom) lives next

    door.

2. Having lived in the apartment long before (he / him), I insisted that I

    could better judge (who / whom) the stereo would disturb.

3. A rabid advocate of tenants' rights, he believed that (we / us) renters had the right to do whatever we chose to do in our apartments.

4. I reminded him that *our* rights were probably in conflict with (them / those) of the people (who / whom) lived around us.

5. "Besides," I said, "the rules about loud music are not for (us / we) tenants to decide; Mr. Ronan, the landlord, spelled out the rules to you and (I / me) when we signed the lease."

6. Enraged, he insisted that (he / him) and (I / me) should discuss the matter with Mr. Ronan.

7. Just then the phone rang; it was the building manager, (who / whom) had warned us about loud music twice before.

8. A moment later there was a knock on the door. "(Whom / Who) in the heck is that?" yelled my roommate.

9. "It is (I / me)," said the student (who / whom) lived next door, a pompous fellow who spent most of his time correcting my roommate's grammar. My roommate opened the door in a fit of rage.

10. Standing beside two police officers, our pompous neighbor said to us, "It is time for you and (I / me) to have a talk."

11. "Your music," said one of the officers, "is disturbing (him / his) studying."

12. As it turned out, our neighbor hadn't even filed a complaint against my roommate and (I / me).

13. The building manager said that (he / him) and his wife had heard the music in their apartment, three flights down.

14. One of the police officers said that (she / her) and her partner had heard the music from the street.

15. My roommate and (I / me) moved out the next week.

13

Pronoun Reference

13–1 Using Personal Pronouns Consistently (*RHH,* 13a)

In the following passages, change all personal pronouns from first to third person. After you have done so, read each passage carefully, making sure that all pronouns are consistent. How does the change from the first to third person affect each passage? What advantage, if any, does the author gain by using first person? One pronoun in each passage is done for you as an example.

PASSAGE 1

When *he* ~~I~~ wrote the following pages, or rather the bulk of them, I lived alone, in the woods, a mile from any neighbor, in a house which I had built myself, on the shore of Walden Pond, in Concord, Massachusetts, and earned my living by the labor of my hands only.—*Henry David Thoreau*[13]

PASSAGE 2

She

~~I~~ had awakened at five and decided to fish for a few hours. I rowed
the dinghy out to the boat on that lovely foggy morning and then
headed around my side of Martha's Vineyard into the heavy waters
of West Chop. Up toward Lake Tashmoo I found the quiet rip where
5   the flounders had been running, put out two lines, and made myself
some coffee.—*Lillian Hellman*[14]

13–2 Revising Abrupt Pronoun Shifts
(*RHH,* 13a)

The following sentences contain a common type of abrupt pronoun shift—personal pronouns that fail to agree in number with the indefinite pronouns that serve as their antecedents. Revise each sentence in the space provided, making pronouns agree with their antecedents and avoiding the use of "he" to refer to both men and women. Often, the best solution is to recast the entire sentence.

Example: Everyone has a right to their own opinion.

Everyone has the right to an opinion.

1. None of the students volunteered their time for the fundraiser.

2. Anybody should be able to solve the puzzle by themselves.

3. One of these kids is doing their own thing.—*Sesame Street*

4. Each student was given the choice of three writing topics.

5. Someone had their phone number carved in the top of the desk.

_____

_____

13–3 Identifying and Eliminating Problems in Pronoun Reference (*RHH*, 13b–g)

In the following sentences, cross out any pronoun that does not agree in number with its antecedent. Write the correct pronoun in the space provided. If a sentence contains no error, write C in the space.

Example: Elephants use their trunks to carry water to

their mouths and to hose it~~self~~ down.   *themselves*

1. In the wild, African elephants feed mainly on grass, but they will eat dozens of other foods as well.   _____

2. The Asian elephant, on the other hand, eats from the trees and bushes found in their native forests.   _____

3. Neither the African nor the Asian elephant digests their food very efficiently.   _____

4. In fact, every elephant consumes about double the amount of food their body actually needs.   _____

5. Anyone interested in keeping an elephant as a pet would certainly find themselves with an enormous grocery bill; a pair of elephants in the backyard would probably consume about a quarter of a million pounds of food a year.   _____

6. Elephants use their trunks to feed itself.   _____

7. An African elephant has two "fingers" at the end of its trunk; it uses these in feeding.   _____

8. These fingers are so flexible that the elephant can use it to pick a single leaf. _____

9. Their tusks also help an elephant find food. _____

10. The tusks serve as probes; with it the elephant digs roots out of the earth and finds water in the river-beds, even when they are completely dry. _____

13–4 Revising Sentences for Pronoun Agreement (*RHH,* 13b–g)

Revise the following sentences, using the directions given in parentheses. Make all changes necessary to bring pronouns into agreement with their antecedents and verbs with their subjects. Other changes may also be necessary. Make your revisions in the space above the lines.

Example: My color-blind interior ~~decorator is~~ using ~~his~~ favorite shade of purple to redecorate my living room. (Change *decorator* to *decorators.*)

(handwritten above: decorators are their)

1. People who live in glass houses should leave their clothes on. (Change *People* to *Anyone.*)

2. Either Bridget or Nora must decide whether she plans to sing "Who Put the Overalls in Mrs. Murphy's Chowder" at next week's Irish song-fest. (Delete *Either;* change *or* to *and.*)

3. Kevin had no trouble deciding that he would do his famous imitation of Richard Nixon singing "When Irish Eyes Are Smiling." (Change *Kevin* to *The O'Meara brothers.*)

4. The legislature finally took the courageous step we had all been waiting for, giving its full suppot to the banning of pay toilets. (Change *legislature* to *legislator.*)

5. Every dog will have its day. (Change *Every* to *All.*)

13–5 Pronoun Reference: Clarifying Antecedents (*RHH*, 13b–g)

In each of the following passages, underline any pronoun that lacks a clear, explicit antecedent. Then, in the space above the lines, make whatever changes are needed to correct the problem. In some cases you may have to supply antecedents.

Example: Tomatoes were once believed to be poison. ~~In Europe they~~ *Europeans* grew

them as a curiosity before <u>they</u> grew them as a food.

1. Primitive people often used vegetables in their fertility rites. This survives today in our marriage custom of throwing rice on newlyweds.

2. Instead of rice, some Europeans use peas. They throw it into the bride's lap, which increases her fertility—at least according to folklore.

3. They say that eating carrots improves one's eyesight. It is probably not just a myth.

4. Carrots do, in fact, have a high vitamin A content. This is known to help correct the problem of night blindness.

5. Some vegetables, including asparagus and onions, were once thought to be aphrodisiacs. They were eaten to stimulate their ardor for lovemaking.

13–6 Review Exercise: Editing a Passage to Eliminate Problems in the Use of Pronouns (*RHH*, 12a–i, 13a–g)

Edit the following paragraphs to eliminate problems with pronoun case and reference. Underline any pronoun that is in the wrong case; that lacks a clear, explicit antecedent; or that fails to agree with its antecedent. Make the necessary changes in the space above the lines. The first sentence is edited for you as an example.[15]

People

~~They~~ discovered cucumbers in India thousands of years ago. It

was later grown by Greeks and Romans whom used forcing techniques for a year-round crop. Columbus brought it to America on one of their early voyages, and they gradually spread throughout the New World.

In Buddhist lore it symbolized fertility. Egyptians and Jews delighted in the refreshing fruit. This was not true of the English, whom remained fearful of its "natural coldness" for centuries. (This is caused by its high water content.) Early American settlers believed that dreaming about the cucumber when one was ill would bring them good health, and that a person whom ate cucumbers would have a sharper appetite. They also applied it in ointment form to soothe and cool the skin.

14

Parallelism

Note: The following exercises are designed to help you locate and correct faulty parallelism. For practice in using parallelism to make your writing more effective, see Exercises 7–18, 7–19, and 7–20, pages 154–158.

14–1 Identifying Correct Parallel Construction
(*RHH,* 14a)

Decide which sentence in each pair contains a *correct* parallel construction. Circle the letter of the correct sentence, and underline its parallel elements.

Example: (a) Critics of "plastic money" believe that credit cards have become too easy to get and too painless to use.

(b) Critics of "plastic money" believe that credit cards have become too easy to get and are too painless to use.

1. (a) Major credit companies earn millions of dollars each year from consumers who prefer to buy now and later to pay the bills.

   (b) Major credit companies earn millions of dollars each year from consumers who prefer to buy now and pay later.

2. (a) Widely accepted both in the United States and abroad, credit cards enable users to travel with ease, to eat at the best restaurants, and to shop at the finest stores.

   (b) Widely accepted both in the United States and abroad, credit cards enable users to travel with ease, eating at the best restaurants, and to shop at the finest stores.

3. (a) Nowadays credit cards are used not only to purchase luxury items but also to buy essential services.

   (b) Nowadays credit cards not only are used to purchase luxury items but also to buy essential services.

4. (a) For example, some hospitals now display signs inviting patients to pay either with MasterCard or with Visa.

   (b) For example, some hospitals now display signs inviting patients to pay either with MasterCard or paying with Visa.

5. (a) Some complain that the ease of using a credit card now exceeds the ease of cash.

   (b) Some complain that the ease of using a credit card now exceeds the ease of using cash.

14–2 Identifying and Revising Faulty Parallelism (*RHH*, 14a–h)

In the following sentences, underline any instances of faulty parallelism. Then revise the problem, writing your correction in the space above the lines. Circle the number of any sentence that requires no revision.

Examples: ① Most people drink milk for its taste, not for its health benefits.

2. Even those who dislike the taste of milk consume it whenever
   a variety of other
   they eat butter, cheese, ice cream, and ~~eating a variety of other~~
   foods.
   ~~foods.~~

1. The Jersey, a fawn-colored cow, and the Holstein, a black and white cow, are among the most popular dairy breeds.

2. Milk varies in color and composition, depending on the breed of cow and the nature of its diet.

3. For example, the milk of Holsteins is whiter than Jerseys'.

4. Whichever breed produces it, cows' milk is a nearly ideal food, containing fats, proteins, carbohydrates, and it contains several vitamins and minerals.

5. Virtually all milk sold in the United States is both pasteurized and it is homogenized.

6. During pasteurization, milk is heated to destroy disease-causing organisms and to eliminate some of the bacteria that promote souring.

7. Developed and named after Louis Pasteur in the 1860s, pasteurization helped control the spread of tuberculosis.

8. Today, pasteurization may seem more a precaution, rather than a necessity, but even with modern handling methods, some nonpasteurized milk would undoubtedly become contaminated.

9. Unlike pasteurization, homogenization is not so much a necessity, but rather a convenience.

10. Whether necessary or it is not necessary, the homogenization process is used widely in the United States.

11. Homogenized milk is blended so thoroughly that its cream will not separate and rising to the top.

12. Long before they knew about pasteurization and homogenization, people drank milk; they also used it to make butter, cheese, and yogurt.

13. Milk can, and indeed always has been, used to make such products.

14. Today most Americans, and indeed most people throughout the world, drink cows' milk.

15. But in some countries, other animals provide part of the milk supply: the buffalo in India, the goat in several Mediterranean countries, and in northern Europe reindeers are still used for milk.

14-3 Punctuating Parallel Elements
(*RHH*, 14i-l)

The following sentences (adapted from the Declaration of Independence) contain some parallel elements that require punctuation and others that are punctuated unnecessarily. Add commas where appropriate and circle any punctuation that should be omitted.[16]

Example: He has forbidden his Government to pass laws of immediate͜and pressing importance.

1. We hold these truths to be self-evident that all men are created equal, that they are endowed by their Creator with certain unalienable Rights that among these are Life Liberty and the Pursuit of Happiness.

2. The history of the present King of Great Britain is a history of repeated injuries, and usurpations.

3. He has called together legislative bodies at places unusual uncomfortable and distant from the depository of their Public Records.

4. He has plundered our seas ravaged our Coasts burnt our towns, and destroyed the lives of our people.

5. We have reminded them of the circumstances of our immigration, and settlement here.

15

Relations between Tenses

15-1 Establishing Correct Relationships between Tenses within a Sentence (*RHH*, 15a–b)

In each of the following sentences, circle any verb whose tense is not properly related to the tense of the underlined verb. Then write the correct verb form in the space provided. If the sentence contains no error, write C in the space.[17]

Example: *The Book of Lists* <u>includes</u> an entry

that ⬭described⬭ fifteen well-known

love offerings   *describes*

1. When his wife <u>died</u> in 1631, Shah Jahnan,

   emperor of the Moguls, builds the

   magnificent Taj Mahal in her honor.   _____

2. After Marc Antony and Cleopatra <u>became</u> lovers, he presents her with Cyprus, Phoenicia, Coele-Syria, and parts of Arabia, Cilicia, and Judea.

_____

3. Since most present-day lovers <u>own</u> far less real estate than Marc Antony, they had to give more modest gifts.

_____

4. Richard Burton, however, gives several love offerings that <u>would have impressed</u> Cleopatra herself.

_____

5. Elizabeth Taylor <u>was given</u> a $1,050,000 gem that Burton has purchased from Cartier.

_____

6. "Diamond Jim" Brady <u>gave</u> actress Lillian Russell a gold-plated bicycle; its spokes have been encrusted with chips of diamonds, emeralds, rubies, and sapphires.

_____

7. When Russell <u>went</u> on tour, the bicycle—kept in an expensive morocco case—travels with her.

_____

8. Most lovers, of course, <u>cannot afford</u> a gold-plated bicycle (or an ordinary ten-speed, for that matter), so they gave more modest gifts.

_____

9. Most of us <u>settle</u> for a box of candy or a

dozen roses, or we took our beloved

out for a fancy dinner. _____

10. But just in case we do <u>strike</u> it rich, *The*

Book of Lists offers a few suggestions

for more expensive gifts. _____

15–2 Changing the Governing Tense of a Passage (*RHH,* 15a–b)

Edit the following passage so that its governing tense is past rather than present. Make sure that the tense of every verb is correctly related to the tense of the first verb, which has been changed for you as an example.

> *was*
> It i̶s̶ long past midnight when she arrives at the Hotel Thompson
> which stands like the only living thing in the shuttered street. Lise
> parks the little black car in a spot near the entrance, takes her book
> and her zipper-bag and enters the hall.
> 5   At the desk the night-porter is on duty, the top three buttons of
> his uniform unfastened to reveal his throat and the top of his under-
> vest, a sign that the deep night has fallen and the tourists have gone
> to bed. The porter is talking on the desk telephone which links with
> the bedrooms. Meanwhile the only other person in the hall, a young-
> 10   ish man in a dark suit, stands before the desk with a brief-case and a
> tartan hold-all by his side.—*Muriel Spark*[18]

15–3 Matching Verb Forms to a Governing Tense (*RHH,* 15a–b)

In the space provided, change each verb in parentheses to its correct form. Make sure that all verbs are consistent with the governing tense established in the first sentence. One verb is supplied for you as an example.

Every day, during breaks and after lunch, Speyer fed bits of bacon to the blue lizards that (live) 1.___*lived*___ outside the barracks. He soon (concentrate) 2._____ on one bold lizard, and after a week he (have) 3._____ us as an audience. Sitting on the barracks steps, he (put) 4._____ his hand on the ground, palm up. He then (set) 5._____ bacon pieces in it, placing more in the crook of his arm and on his shoulder. Soon the lizard (come) 6._____ from under the steps, moving quickly, then stopping to do a sort of push-up and pant in its throat like a frog. It (take) 7._____ the food in his palm, then (run) 8._____ easily up to his elbow and finally all the way to his shoulder.

After a few days, we (press) 9._____ Speyer to expand his performance. During afternoon break, he (repeat) 10._____ the usual sequence. But this time, as the lizard (eat) 11._____ from his shoulder, Speyer slowly (turn) 12._____ his face to it. Tensed to run, the lizard suddenly (thrust) 13._____ its body toward Speyer's extended tongue. It (come) 14._____ away with a shred of bacon, then (flash) 15._____ down his arm and out of sight.—*Miles Wilson*[19]

15–4 Correcting Shifts in Verb Tense within a Passage (*RHH*, 15a–b)

The following paragraph contains unacceptable shifts in verb tense. Correct any verb that does not follow in a correct sequence from the tense established at the beginning of the passage. One verb is corrected for you as an example.[20]

A fertilized female tarantula lays from 200 to 400 eggs at a time;

thus it ~~was~~ *is* possible for a single tarantula to produce several thousand

young. She takes no care of them beyond weaving a cocoon of silk to

have enclosed the eggs. After they hatched, the young walked away,

5   found convenient places in which to dig their burrows and spend the

rest of their lives in solitude. Tarantulas feed mostly on insects and

millipedes. Once their appetite was appeased, they digest the food

for several days before eating again. Their sight is poor, being lim-

ited to sensing a change in the intensity of light and to the perception

10   of moving objects. They apparently had little or no sense of hearing,

for a hungry tarantula would have paid no attention to a loudly chirp-

ing cricket placed in its cage unless the insect happens to touch one

of its legs.

15–5 Using Verb Tense in Direct and Indirect Discourse (*RHH*, 15d–e)

Rewrite the following quotations as indirect discourse. Make sure that you change verb tenses as necessary.

Example: "I have decided not to return to college this term," said Hamlet.

> *Hamlet said that he had decided not to return to college this term.*

1. "I never wanted to go to college in Germany in the first place," he protested.

\
\

2. "I plan to go to a vocational school where I can pick up a useful trade," he said.

\
\

237

3. "I have had it with the curriculum at Wittenberg," he insisted.

_____

_____

4. "No matter what Uncle Claudius wants," he added, "I will study clothmaking."

_____

_____

5. "If I had worked at the trade since boyhood, I would be a master clothmaker today," he concluded.

_____

_____

15–6 Review Exercise: Editing a Passage for Errors in Parallel Construction and Shifts in Verb Tense (*RHH*, 14a–j, 15a–h)

Edit the following passage to eliminate errors in parallel construction (including faulty punctuation) and shifts in verb tense. Make the necessary changes in the space above the lines. You may want to copy your revised version onto a separate sheet of paper before submitting it. Two errors are corrected for you as an example.*

       Every serious student can expect to write a major research proj-

ect at one time or another during her academic career. Planning,

organizing, and ~~to write~~ *writing* such a paper ~~was~~ *is* an invaluable experience. It

not only gave a student practice in research and writing, but also

5   self-confidence is promoted as the student develops the ability to com-

plete a major task. However, the student is likely to appreciate these

benefits only after the paper is finished. During the course of the

research and while she was writing the paper, the student can expect to

spend an enormous amount of time, and energy. She may also

10   experience a great deal of worry and could be frustrated as well. But

these problems diminish if the student had organized her time wisely, and effectively gathered material.

So far during my college career, I have written my research papers at the last possible moment. However, with the size, and importance of the project I am now doing, continuing this practice would mean a poor performance a case of ulcers and I would probably end up with a low grade. Obviously, to plan carefully and pacing my work was more productive than a last-minute effort. Since my main problem with writing a paper is managing my time efficiently, I planned to make a definite schedule for this project, planning each phase of my research, and to start my writing as early as possible.

PUNCTUATION

16

Period,
Question Mark,
Exclamation Point

16-1 Using Periods, Question Marks,
and Exclamation Points (*RHH,* 16a–j)

Some of the following sentences contain errors in the use of periods, question marks, and exclamation points. Correct the errors in the space above the lines. Circle the number of any sentence that is punctuated correctly.

Example: "Will having an M.B.A. help you find a better job?" I asked.

1. Last year I asked my business professor why she had resigned from the college faculty?

2. She said that she planned to return to graduate school.

3. "Why," I asked?

4. She explained that she could eventually earn more money working in industry than she could in teaching, especially if she had an M.B.A.

5. I told her that I was surprised (!) to learn that business people made more than college professors.

6. She laughed.

7. I asked her how she planned to make a living while earning an M.B.A.?

8. She said "night school," thought for a minute, and then made a strange remark.

9. Was she merely pulling my leg when she asked, "Do you think I can get a part-time job as a plumber or an actress?"?

10. A year later I saw her on a television advertisement for Comet cleanser; she was playing the part of Josephine the Plumber.

17

Comma

17-1 Using Commas to Join Independent Clauses (*RHH*, 17a)

Underline all coordinating conjunctions in the following sentences. Then insert a comma before each conjunction that joins two *independent clauses*. Circle any commas that are used incorrectly between coordinating elements.[1]

Example: More than forty species of termites can be found in the United States⊙and Canada, <u>but</u> the most destructive is the subterranean termite.

1. These voracious insects are often called white ants yet their appearance is actually very different from that of the ant.

2. The body of the termite is comparatively straight, and of approximately equal thickness throughout its length.

3. The ant has a narrow-waisted body that is shaped like an hourglass, and hind wings that are shorter than its forewings.

4. Termites live off of cellulose, or rotting plant material in the soil but they also attack wooden objects such as house timbers or furniture.

5. In colder climates the subterranean termite stays below the frost line, and can live for as long as ten months without a taste of the cellulose found in wood but in areas where there is no frost it can eat the year round.

6. This species is especially fond of softwoods such as pine but it will just as eagerly attack any type of wood.

7. The destruction wrought by termites is hidden from view, and may take place slowly over a long period of time but it can be devastatingly thorough.

8. Termites eat only the interior sections of a timber or they hollow out a piece of furniture, leaving just a shell.

9. They often go undetected for no opening ever shows on the surface of the wood they attack.

10. Worker termites cannot endure exposure to light, and open air so they often build mud tunnels from the ground to a new source of food.

17-2 Sentence Practice: Using Commas to Join Independent Clauses (*RHH*, 17a)

Write five sentences in which you use a comma and the conjunction in parentheses to join two independent clauses. (Suggested topics for your sentences: fast-food restaurants, politics, your home town)

Example: (yet) *The senator claimed that he had no interest in the nomination, yet he continued to promote speculation about his candidacy.*

1. (and) _____

   _____

   _____

2. (but) _____

   _____

   _____

3. (or) _____

   _____

   _____

4. (for) _____

   _____

   _____

5. (so) _____

   _____

   _____

17–3   Using Commas to Set Off Introductory Elements (*RHH,* 17d–e)

In the following sentences, add commas where necessary to set off introductory modifying elements—words, phrases, or clauses. Consider the comma optional if the introductory element is brief and if the sentence is clear without the added comma.

Example: Like bees and ants, termites are social insects.

1. Highly organized they live in colonies consisting of a queen, winged reproductives, soldiers, and workers.

2. During her lifespan of forty years or more a single queen lays millions of eggs.

3. In one day she may produce as many as 35,000.

4. Although they are blind, sterile, and unable to stand exposure to light or dryness worker termites can be incredibly destructive.

5. In nature they enrich the soil by speeding the decay of vegetable matter.

6. Unfortunately they are not discriminating.

7. When conditions are right they will invade the timbers in a home just as readily as they will a rotting stump in the woods.

8. Building tunnels they work steadily and methodically, destroying support timbers, framing lumber, or even the paper surface on sheetrock.

9. Causing extensive damage each year in the United States they cost homeowners millions of dollars.

10. Although few people realize it homeowners pay far more each year to repair termite damage than they do to repair the ravages of hurricanes and tornadoes.

17-4 Sentence Practice: Using Commas to Set Off Introductory Elements (*RHH*, 17d-e)

Write five sentences in which you use commas to set off the type of introductory element named in parentheses. (Suggested topics for your sentences: pressures on college students, the expense of raising children, television commercials)

Example: (phrase) *Along with the pressure to do well academically, most students feel a great deal of pressure to succeed socially.*

(clause) *If raising children is expensive today, imagine what the costs will be twenty years from now.*

(word) *Nevertheless, most people still say they want to have children, despite the cost.*

1. (phrase) _____

_____

_____

2. (phrase) _____

_____

_____

3. (clause) _____

_____

_____

4. (clause) _____

_____

_____

5. (word) _____

_____

_____

17–5 Using Commas with Nonrestrictive Elements (*RHH,* 17f–i)

In the following sentences, add commas where necessary to set off nonrestrictive elements, including sentence adverbs, transitional expressions, appositives, and parenthetical elements. Underline any material that you set off. Then circle commas that are used incorrectly to set off restrictive elements. Finally, circle the number of any sentence that is punctuated correctly.[2]

Examples: (a) Africanized bees, which have devastated the beekeeping industry in many Latin American countries, continue to move toward the United States.

(b) There is growing concern among the 200,000 people, who raise bees in the United States.

1. Killer bees the Africanized honeybees that have stung hundreds of people to death in recent years have just entered Costa Rica on their steady move north.

2. The scientists, who have been studying Africanized bees, predict that they will arrive in the United States by the end of the decade.

3. In 1957, twenty-six swarms of African queen bees, which are more aggressive than European varieties, escaped from a laboratory in São Paulo, Brazil.

4. The African bees rapidly took over docile bee colonies, that lived in the region.

5. According to David Roubik a Smithsonian bee biologist most colonies along the Atlantic coast of South America are now Africanized.

6. There are claims Roubik up to 300,000 bees per square mile.

7. Africanized bees look just like the European bees, that are common in the United States.

8. They are however much more likely to react to an intruder.

9. In fact, they react up to thirty times more quickly and are up to ten times more likely to sting.

10. Some scientists doubt whether the killer bees accustomed to the warm southern climate will be able to withstand northern temperatures, and others contend that the bees will become gentler as they interbreed with European varieties.

17–6 Sentence Practice: Using Commas with Nonrestrictive Elements (*RHH,* 17f–i)

Write five sentences using correctly punctuated nonrestrictive elements. (Suggested topics for your sentences: popular music and musicians, home cooking)

Example: <u>The bass player, a distinguished -</u>
<u>looking man, with a Mohawk</u>
<u>haircut, jumped onto the stage</u>
<u>from a suspended platform.</u>

1. _____

_____

_____

2. _____

_____

_____

3. _____

_____

_____

4. _____

_____

_____

5. _____

_____

_____

17–7 Using Commas to Separate Coordinate Modifiers and Items in a Series (*RHH*, 17j, n)

In the following passages, supply commas where necessary to separate coordinate modifiers and items in a series. (The passages are adapted from an 1898 book of advice for young women.)[3]

PASSAGE 1

I knew one girl, supposed to be a very fine student, who brought

on "fits" by overstudy while away at college. I had the opportunity

251

to investigate this sad disheartening case, and I discovered that she had been eating from morning till night. She carried nuts candy and apples in her pocket and pickles and cake in her room and studied and munched until it was no doubt a disturbed digestion rather than an overused brain that caused the "fits."

PASSAGE 2

If you eat regularly of plain meat vegetables fruits cereals milk and eggs, and if you avoid rich pastries cakes puddings pickles and sweetmeats, you will have compassed the round of healthful wholesome diet. I would like to emphasize the fact, however, that tea and coffee are not foods. They are irritants stimulants nerve-poisons. If you are wise you will avoid them. You will also avoid the use of alcohol in all forms, whether wine ales beer or cider.

17–8 Sentence Practice: Using Commas to Separate Items in a Series and Coordinate Modifiers (*RHH,* 17j, n)

Write three sentences using commas to separate items in a series and two sentences using commas between coordinate modifiers. (Suggested topics for your sentences: favorite desserts, flowers, famous quarterbacks)

Examples: (series) *The senator promised to have the tulip declared the state flower, an endangered species, and a national treasure.*

(coordinate modifiers) *The sundae was topped with a puff of rich, thick whipped cream.*

1. (series) _____

_____

_____

252

2. (series) _____

_____

_____

3. (series) _____

_____

_____

4. (coordinate modifiers) _____

_____

_____

5. (coordinate modifiers) _____

_____

_____

17–9 Review Exercise: Editing a Passage for Comma Errors (*RHH,* 17a–o)

Edit the following passages by adding commas where necessary and circling those that are not needed. The first sentence is done for you as an example. (Some commas are used correctly; some are optional.)[4]

PASSAGE 1

The oceans' legendary mists have long swirled with tales of exotic beasts but stories, whether based on fact or fantasy, tell of no creature⊙ with as much age-old charm⊙ as the mermaid. The idea of near-humans—both male and female—inhabiting the sea, and inland waters

5 has captured imagination since people first ventured seaward and for a very long time mermaids seemed every bit as real, as flying fish.

PASSAGE 2

The folklore of mermaids is ancient, and widespread crossing cultures continents and centuries. Mer-people have been called by diverse names—Sirens nixies and Nereids among others.

253

PASSAGE 3

Like all folkloric characters, each group of mer-people has specific traits, and habitats but there are some features, that we have come to associate with the generic mermaid. The part-woman part-fish charmer gives room for a great deal of artistic variation, but most
5   mermaids tend to merge woman with fish near, or below the waist. At that point, the torso starts to taper with scaly grace to a fish's tail.

PASSAGE 4

In overall form their bodies are designed for open-water seductions, and quick getaways, and mermaids are as the story goes as soulless as water. Traditionally the only way for a mermaid to acquire a soul, is by marrying a mortal.

PASSAGE 5

The moon goddess Atargatis known also as Derceto and worshiped by Syrians Philistines and Israelites is the earliest female fish deity. As a moon goddess Atargatis added many facets to the fish-god profile. She was associated with the more mysterious attributes of the
5   night, and she went on to acquire an aura of seductiveness vanity beauty cruelty and unattainable love.

PASSAGE 6

There has always been a discrepancy in the descriptions of the mermaids cited by naturalists, and sea captains and those representing the poetic truths of artists. Compare for example the lovely sea-maid of "dulcet breath" that Shakespeare wrote of in *A Midsummer*
5   *Night's Dream* with the Amboina Mermaid, that appeared in natural history volumes in the early 1700s. Although the mermaid of Amboina is given the glamour of exotic coloring she is still described as

a monster. In an original color drawing by Samuel Fallours published
in 1717 she has copper-colored skin highlighted with a green, that

10   matches the hula skirt of fins around her hips.

PASSAGE 7

By the middle of the 19th century stuffed mermaids had become
spectacles in Victorian London. Showmen bought most of these so-
called preserved specimens usually trumped-up monkey-fish com-
posites from Japanese fishermen.

PASSAGE 8

The vitality of the mermaid legend indicates, that there may be a
substratum of fact an animal that may appear mermaidlike, from a
distance. Several possibilities have been suggested: the sea cows of
the order Sirenia, including the manatee and the dugong, and, of

5   course, the many varieties of seals.

PASSAGE 9

While these animals hardly have the beauty to sink a ship, or even attract a sailor long at sea they do have certain characteristics similar
to those ascribed to mermaids. The nearly hairless manatee is somewhat larger than the human female but the female manatee's breasts

5   which are forward near its flipperlike forelimbs are in a position
similar to the human female's. The manatee has no other limbs and
its blubbery body tapers to a horizontal flipper of a tail. The dugong
is similar in shape to the manatee. It has a muzzle covered with bristly
whiskers, and is said to suckle its young with its upper body out of

10   the water cradling the baby with one flipper.

18
Semicolon and Colon

SEMICOLON

18–1 Using Semicolons (*RHH,* 18a–d)

In the following passages, decide whether semicolons are used correctly. If the semicolon is correct, write C in the space provided; if it is incorrect, write X. Be prepared to explain which mark of punctuation, if any, should replace each semicolon that you mark incorrect.[5]

Example: Most of the dead animals you see on highways near the cities are dogs; a few cats.   *X*

1. Out in the countryside, the forms and coloring of the dead are strange; these are the wild creatures. _____

2. Seen from a car window, they appear as fragments, evoking memories of woodchucks, badgers, skunks, voles, snakes; sometimes the mysterious wreckage of a deer. _____

3. It is always a queer shock, part a sudden welling of grief; part unaccountable amazement. _____

4. It is simply astounding; to see an animal dead on a highway. _____

5. The outrage is more than just the location; it is the impropriety of such visible death, anywhere. _____

6. You do not expect to see dead animals in the open; it is the nature of animals to die alone, off somewhere, hidden. _____

7. It is wrong to see them lying out on the highway; it is wrong to see them anywhere. _____

8. Everything in the world dies. We only know about it; however, as a kind of abstraction. _____

9. If you stand in a meadow, at the edge of a hillside, and look around carefully; almost everything you can catch sight of is in the process of dying, and most things will be dead long before you are. _____

10. If it were not for the constant renewal and replacement going on before your eyes; the whole place would turn to stone and sand under your feet. _____

18-2 Sentence Practice: Using Semicolons (*RHH*, 18a–d)

Write two sentences of your own using semicolons to link closely related independent clauses. Then write three sentences in which you join independent clauses by using a semicolon and the sentence adverb given in parentheses. (Suggested topics for your sentences: teachers, the perfect vacation, writing)

Examples: (related clauses) *There were fifty people waiting in line; every one of them wanted to sign up for Ms. Tilka's advanced writing course.*

(moreover) *Ms. Tilka was an immensely popular teacher; moreover, her students usually finished her course well prepared to write in their other courses.*

1. (related clauses) _____

   _____

   _____

   _____

2. (related clauses) _____

   _____

   _____

   _____

3. (therefore) _____

   _____

   _____

   _____

4. (however) _____

   _____

   _____

   _____

5. (furthermore) _____

   _____

   _____

   _____

18–3 Using Semicolons for Special Effects (*RHH,* 18a–d)

Study the use of semicolons in the following passages. Be prepared to discuss why the semicolon is an effective choice for the context in which it appears. Using your own paper, rewrite each passage to eliminate all semicolons. How does your revision change the author's intended effect?

1. Once great men created fortunes; today a great system creates fortunate men.—*Richard Hofstadter*[6]

2. When I'm through in the bakery, I have the choice of (1) going to my cell; (2) staying in the dining room to watch TV; (3) going down to the library; or (4) going out to the yard to walk around, sit in the sun, lift weights, play some funny game. . . .—*Eldridge Cleaver*[7]

3. The period tells you that that is that; if you didn't get all the meaning you wanted or expected, anyway you got all the writer intended to parcel out and now you have to move along. But with a semicolon there you get a pleasant little feeling of expectancy; there is more to come; read on; it will get clearer.—*Lewis Thomas*[8]

COLON

18-4 Using Colons (*RHH,* 18e–i)

In the following passages, decide whether colons are used correctly. If the colon is correct, write C in the space provided; if it is incorrect, write X. Be prepared to explain which mark of punctuation, if any, should replace each colon that you mark incorrect.

Example: Before deciding to major in English, I had tried: **X**
psychology, anthropology, and geography.   _____

1. As an academic discipline, anthropology has its attractions: an intriguing combination of book learning and field work.   _____

2. I was concerned, however: that a degree in anthropology might make it difficult for me to get a job after graduation.   _____

3. A degree in psychology, on the other hand, can lead to several careers, such as: social work, counseling, or teaching.   _____

4. The two "tracks" offered by the geography department were: physical geography and human geography, but neither appealed to me.   _____

5. I finally decided that the English department's program had the kind of variety I wanted: courses in literature, language, creative writing, and professional writing.   _____

18-5 Using Colons to Achieve Economy
(*RHH*, 18e–i)

Rewrite the following passages, using a colon and a list to make each passage more economical. Use your own paper.

Example: Mrs. Goodnight's living room was legendary. It was a bizarre swirl of clashing colors. There were red drapes. On the drapes were chartreuse ties. The walls were a dingy orange. The carpet was a war between lavender and peach.

> *Mrs. Goodnight's legendary living room was a swirl of clashing colors: red drapes with chartreuse ties, dingy orange walls, and a carpet on which lavender fought with peach.*

1. Professor Wilson planned to assign four novels in his pop-lit course. The class would read Owen Wister's *The Virginian*. They would also read Margaret Mitchell's *Gone with the Wind*. And they would read Harriet Beecher Stowe's *Uncle Tom's Cabin* and James Michener's *Poland*.

2. The mayor outlined three major problems that the town had to address. There was an inadequate sewer system. Also, the city needed to replace its outdated fire fighting equipment. Finally, something had to be done to upgrade police protection.

18-6 Sentence Practice: Using Colons
(*RHH*, 18e–i)

Write three sentences in which you use colons. (Suggested topics for your sentences: shoes, popular magazines, ice cream flavors)

Example: *Converse tennis shoes have the features that everyone wants: comfort, style, and the right price.*

1. _____

_____

_____

_____

2. _____

_____

_____

_____

3. _____

_____

_____

_____

19

Dash
and
Parentheses

19–1 Using Dashes (*RHH*, 19a–e)

Write five sentences of your own showing the correct use of the dash. Two of your sentences should contain paired dashes. (Suggested topics for your sentences: books, inexpensive ways to travel, grandparents)

Example: (paired dashes)   *Jane's latest novel — a murder mystery — was selling very poorly according to her publisher.*

1. (dash) _____

_____

_____

2. (dash) _____

_____

_____

3. (dash) _____

_____

_____

_____

4. (paired dashes) _____

_____

_____

_____

5. (paired dashes) _____

_____

_____

_____

19–2 Using Parentheses (*RHH,* 19f–j)

Write three sentences that illustrate the correct use of parentheses. (Suggested topics for your sentences: sports fans, world leaders, your home state or province)

Example: Canadian prime minister Lester Pearson (1897–1972) received the Nobel Peace Prize for his role in mediating the 1956 Arab-Israeli War.

1. _____

_____

_____

_____

2. _____

_____

_____

_____

3. _____

_____

_____

_____

19–3 Review Exercises: Using Commas, Semicolons, Colons, Dashes, and Parentheses (*RHH*, 17, 18, 19)

For each blank space in the following passages, supply the necessary mark of punctuation: comma, semicolon, colon, dash, or parentheses. If no punctuation is needed, write an X in the space. The first sentence is done for you as an example. (In some cases, more than one mark of punctuation is correct; in others, punctuation is optional.)

PASSAGE 1

While the cowboy sat there quietly tuning his guitar (1)__,__ I marveled at how rough (2)__X__ and weatherbeaten he was. His boots looked as if he had worn them a hundred years (3)_____ the color was faded (4)_____ the leater was scruffed (5)_____ and cracked (6)_____ and the heels were worn almost flat. One pant leg was half tucked into the tall leg of his boot (7)_____ the other extended all the way down to his heel. A dark piece of denim was sewn in place just above his right knee (8)_____ clashing with the dirty (9)_____ light blue color of his jeans. A brand new belt (10)_____ a real contrast to the rest of his outfit (11)_____ hung loosely around his waist (12)_____ practically useless because of the tight fit of his jeans.*

PASSAGE 2

The fact (1)_____ that Epson has sold more printers for more personal computers than all other manufacturers on earth (2)_____ is certainly important to us (3)_____ but why should it matter to you?

The reason we have continually outsold our competition is disarmingly simple (4)_____ we build a better printer for the money.

Epson makes a full line of high-quality printers for every home (5) _____ and business application (6)_____ which is no doubt why computer and software companies (7)_____ as well as other printer companies (8)_____ make their products "Epson-compatible." We're not only the world leader (9)_____ we're the world standard.

Coincidentally (10)_____ another good reason for buying such a widely available printer is that it is widely available.

What's more (11)_____ Epson-brand printers sold in the U.S. are backed by a full one-year warranty (12)_____ on all parts and labor.

And if you *were* to have a problem (13)_____ an unlikely occurrence (14)_____ you could have your Epson serviced at over 1,000 authorized Epson Service Centers (15)_____ from coast to coast.[9]

PASSAGE 3

Several different beverages are in the category of true meads. Strictly speaking (1)_____ mead is made with honey (2)_____ water (3) _____ and yeast. This type of mead may take up to a year to ferment (4) _____ and require up to three years to reach its peak flavor. There are other types of mead (5)_____ just as delicious (6)_____ which are made with fruits. These are known as melomels (7)_____ and they require the same amount of time to ferment (8)_____ and age as our wines. The type of melomels (9)_____ which were once made (10)_____ are as follows (11)_____ pyment (12)_____ a honey wine produced by a combination of honey and grape juice (13)_____ hippocras (14)_____ which is the same as pyment, with spices and herbs added to enhance the flavor (15)_____ metheglin (16)_____ made with honey (17)_____ spices (18)_____ and herbs (19)_____ and cyser, made with honey (20)_____ and apple cider.[10]

20

Quoting

20–1 Using Quotation Marks (*RHH*, 20a–h)

In the following passages, insert quotation marks where necessary.[11]

Example: "The following sentences," said the author, "are adapted from an article in *Saturday Review* called 'What Makes a Genius?' "

1. Just why, asked the law professor, do you say that Rossini was a genius?

2. That's easy, replied the general. He composed a wide variety of great music.

3. That doesn't make him a genius, retorted the editor. He has to have more than great talent and industry to qualify.

4. Well, protested the general, Thomas Wolfe said genius was ninety percent energy and ten percent talent. [The general is paraphrasing Wolfe, not quoting him directly.]

5. Seems to me, remarked the host, that genius is more than what we call talent; genius adds something that wasn't there before.

6. At this point the hostess had found the right page in the dictionary. It says here, she put in, that genius is extraordinary power of invention or origination of any kind. [Beginning with the word *extraordinary,* the hostess quotes directly from the dictionary.]

7. Freud had something to say on the subject, but I'm not sure I can quote him accurately, said the psychoanalyst, blushing a little. As I recall it, he described a genius as something in the nature of one in an hypnotic state, who achieved great things without being really aware of it. [The psychoanalyst does not attempt to quote Freud.]

8. I might go along with that in the arts, said the professor, because I'm sure neither Beethoven nor Van Gogh nor Shakespeare, for example, ever said to himself: Now I'm going to create, now I'm going to perpetrate an act of genius.

9. The editor had been rummaging through his host's books. What about this? he asked. This man Amiel published a diary back in 1850, and he said: Doing easily what others find difficult is talent—doing what is impossible for talent is genius. [The editor quotes Amiel directly.]

10. It's clear enough, said the professor, that not one of us, when the argument started, had more than the foggiest idea of what he meant by the word genius.

20–2 Eliminating Errors in the Use of Quotations (*RHH,* 20a–h, m–p)

Some of the following sentences violate the rules for using double and single quotation marks, ellipsis marks, and brackets. Circle any punctuation that is unnecessary or incorrect. Then add punctuation where appropriate. If a sentence contain no errors, put a check mark before it.

Example: "The movie," said Floyd, " features an actress *{sic}* named Carroll O'Connor."

1. In order to annoy Helen, Tom said, "Shakespeare considered man the superior sex.

2. "In *Hamlet,* he continued, Shakespeare says that *man* is 'the beauty of the world, the paragon of animals.'"

3. Helen said, "Shakespeare no doubt intended to include women in his use of the generic term "man."

4. After she thought for a minute, Helen reminded Tom about *As You Like It:* "In that play Shakespeare makes Rosalind the sensible, level-headed heroine; her lover Orlando acts silly during much of the play."

5. "And in *A Midsummer Night's Dream,*" Helen added, "Bottom says, "*Man* is but an ass."

6. Outwitted, Tom decided to take Helen's advice: 'Read more Shakespeare.'

7. But instead of reading the plays, Tom found a book *about* Shakespeare which said that "the bard wrote more than fifty *(sic)* plays."

8. He also discovered a passage about Shakespeare's female characters: "The bard did, indeed, create many strong . . . portraits of the weaker sex."

9. Helen decided that the book was inaccurate and pompous when she read the following passage: "Shakespeare, that 'sweet swan of Avon,' lived well into the early part of the seventeenth century, writing several novels *(sic)* in addition to his beloved plays . . ."

10. What amused Helen most was the author's statement that ". . . Shakespeare would probably be writing brilliant TV sitcoms if he were alive today."

20–3 Sentence Practice: Integrating Quoted Material (*RHH*, 20i–l)

Using the following guidelines, write five sentences in which you integrate quoted material from a newspaper, magazine, or book. Use your own paper.

1. A sentence in which you integrate a brief quotation so that it does *not* have to be introduced by a comma or a colon

2. A sentence in which you introduce a brief quotation using a comma or a colon

3. A sentence using single quotation marks for a quotation occurring within a quotation

4. A sentence using an ellipsis mark to show that material has been omitted from a quotation

5. A sentence using brackets to insert your own word or words into a quotation

20–4 Combining Quotation Marks with Other Marks of Punctuation (*RHH*, 20f)

In some of the following sentences, quotation marks have been combined incorrectly with other punctuation. Circle each error; then, in the space provided, write the correct punctuation and the word preceding it. If a sentence contains no error, write C in the space.[12]

Example: *Science 84* reports that chemists have discovered a white powder "with a taste more bitter than any known substance on earth(".)   *earth."*

1. The substance is "3,000 times more bitter than quinine."   _____

2. The company that discovered the chemical is "considering putting it in animal repellants or poisons".   _____

3. "No kid will ever drink a bottle of poison with this stuff in it", reported a company official.   _____

4. In *A Distant Mirror,* Barbara W. Tuchman describes the fourteenth century as "a violent, tormented, bewildered, suffering and disintegrating age;" it was "a time, as many thought, of Satan triumphant." _____

5. Tuchman's chapter on the plague of 1348–1350 is called "'This Is the End of the World:' The Black Death." _____

6. The Black Death had reduced the population of Europe "by nearly 50 percent at the end of the century." (Tuchman, p. 119). _____

7. In the country, "peasants dropped dead on the roads, in the fields, in their houses" (Tuchman, p. 98). _____

8. After reading *A Distant Mirror,* Phil asked his history professor, "Is this Tuchman's first book?" _____

9. His professor said, "Don't tell me you've never heard of her other books"! _____

10. "Does the university library have them"? asked Phil. _____

VI

CONVENTIONS

21

Verb Forms

21-1 Using Past Tense and Past Participle Verb Forms (*RHH,* 21a–c)

Circle any incorrect past tense or past participle verb forms in the following sentences. Then write the correct form in the space provided. If a sentence contains no error, write C in the space. Consult a dictionary as necessary to determine the correct forms.

Example: Yesterday I (laid) on the beach for two hours. *lay*

1. Unfortunately, I sat my beach umbrella at the wrong angle; today I'm nursing a sunburn. _____

2. I done the same thing two weeks ago when my friend Joe visited from Galveston. _____

3. We had gone to the beach planning to swim and play volleyball. _____

4. Instead, we set around sunbathing most of the day with a couple of my friends. _____

5. If we had swam, my burn might have been less severe. _____

6. In order to observe wildlife last winter, I built a sturdy, wind-proof shelter in the woods. _____

7. But it didn't seem to help much; every time I used it, my feet and hands were nearly froze. _____

8. Maybe I should have wore warmer clothing. _____

9. But I suppose that after I had sat in near-freezing temperatures for several hours, even the warmest clothing and the best shelter wouldn't have helped. _____

10. Worst of all, I never seen more than a deer or two the entire season. _____

21–2 Using -s and -ed Verb Endings
(RHH, 21a–c)

Circle any verb in the following sentences that lacks a necessary -s or -ed ending. Then write the correct form in the space provided. If a sentence contains no error, write C in the space.

Example: Said Mr. Bunker, "I am not now, nor have I ever been, (prejudice)."   *prejudiced*

1. Mr. Bunker was accustom to his daughter's frequent accusation that he was prejudiced against women. _____

2. "I admit that I use to be prejudiced," he argued, "but I've changed my attitudes." _____

274

3. "I suppose I owe you another chance," said his daughter. _____

4. "I change my views last week," said Mr. Bunker, "after watching a Phil Donahue show that featured a bunch of women-libbers." _____

5. "You're hopeless," his daughter concluded. "The very fact that you used a term like 'women-libbers' shows that you're bias." _____

6. "What am I supposed to call them?" _____

7. "They prefer to be call 'feminists,' and I think you should honor their wishes." _____

8. Alex use to use oil base paint whenever he painted the outside of his house. _____

9. He now prefers latex because it spread more easily and dries more quickly. _____

10. Having just finished a new paint job, he claims that he now see the advantage of aluminum siding. _____

21–3 Identifying Active and Passive Verb Forms (*RHH*, 21b–c)

For each of the following sentences, indicate whether the writer has used an active verb form (A) or a passive verb form (P). Then rewrite each sentence, converting active verbs to passive and passive verbs to active. For sentences that contain passive verbs, you may need to supply subjects (as illustrated in the first example.)*

Examples: It is pointed out in the article that textbooks help teachers organize their courses.   A / Ⓟ

In the article, the author points out that textbooks help teachers organize their courses.

Some teachers regard textbooks as needlessly restrictive. (A)/ P

Textbooks are regarded by some teachers as needlessly restrictive.

1. Homemade teaching materials are preferred by some teachers.   A / P

   _____

   _____

2. The author takes issue with instructors who want to eliminate textbooks.   A / P

   _____

   _____

   _____

3. Because homemade teaching materials are bulky, they often cause storage problems.   A / P

   _____

   _____

   _____

4. Teachers often find textbooks more accessible and simpler to use than homemade materials.   A / P

   _____

   _____

   _____

5. Although textbooks have limitations, many objectives can be achieved by teachers who use them.   A / P

   _____

   _____

   _____

6. With thirty hours of English under my belt, I thought an advanced writing course would be a snap.   A / P

276

7. Errors that I have been making for years are now more easily seen when I edit.   A / P

_____

_____

_____

8. In most of my high school English courses, a formal style of writing was encouraged.   A / P

_____

_____

_____

9. Minor errors can be eliminated through careful proofreading.   A / P

_____

_____

_____

10. I usually write my first drafts very quickly.   A / P

_____

_____

_____

21–4 Converting Verb Forms from Passive to Active (*RHH,* 21b–c)

The following excerpt from Raymond Queneau's *Exercises in Style* illustrates the use of passive voice.[1] Underline the passive verbs. Then rewrite the passage, making all verbs active. The first two sentences are done for you as an example.

It was midday. The bus was being got into by passengers. They

were being squashed together. A hat was being worn on the head of a

277

young gentleman, which hat was encircled by a plait and not by a ribbon. A long neck was one of the characteristics of the young gentleman.

5   The man standing next to him was being grumbled at by the latter because of the jostling which was being inflicted on him by him. As soon as a vacant seat was espied by the young gentleman it was made the object of his precipitate movements and it became sat down upon.

    The young gentleman was later seen by me in front of the gare

10   Saint-Lazare. He was clothed in an overcoat and was having a remark made to him by a friend who happened to be there to the effect that it was necessary to have an extra button put on it.

It was midday. Passengers were getting into the bus.

21-5 Using Subjunctive Verb Forms
(*RHH*, 21d)

Circle any verb in the following sentences that should be subjunctive and is not. Then write the correct subjunctive form in the space provided. If a sentence already contains a correct subjunctive form, write C in the space.

Examples: So be it.   *C*

          Jack wishes he (was) in the land of cotton.   *were*

1. If you have been born in the land of cotton, you too would want to live there.   _____

2. The doctor recommended that Geneva cuts back on her smoking and drinking.   _____

3. She later wished that she had been less forthcoming with the doctor about her vices.   _____

4. The law requires that each eighteen-year-old male registers for the draft.   _____

5. If she had been president, Jane would have vetoed the draft registration bill, a bill she still considers discriminatory.   _____

6. I wish I was finished with this research paper.   _____

7. The instructor requires that everyone submit each paper on or before the due date.   _____

8. It is essential that you are here tomorrow at noon.   _____

9. As Elvis Presley stepped out onto the lawn at Graceland, his fans shouted, "Long lives the king."   _____

10. Let it be.   _____

21–6   Review Exercise: Editing a Passage for Errors in the Use of Verb Forms (*RHH,* 21a–d)

Edit the following passage for errors in past tense, past participle, and subjunctive verb forms. Circle the errors and write your corrections in the space above the lines. The first sentence is done for you as an example.

planted

Last spring my family (plant) a vegetable garden for the first time. At first, everyone was enthusiastic, but since we had all plan a busy summer, we knew the garden would have to be a group effort if it was to succeed.

5   We spent nearly a week planning the project. After we had chose what to grow, we bought seeds and plants at the local feed store. Next, we carefully prepared the soil and lay out the rows using stakes and string. Finally, we planted the seeds and sat out the tomato seedlings.

10   After we finish the planting, my father recommended that each member of the family is in charge of the garden for one month during the summer. Through the end of July, the garden done very well. My brother was then suppose to care for it while the rest of us visited relatives in Idaho. When we return from the trip, we found the gar-

15 den overgrowed with weeds and parched by the August heat. My brother—he lacked the horticultural spirit to start with—had took off unexpectedly, quitting his job to spend the month, as he put it, "on the road getting my head together." He left the garden in charge of a friend who use to live next door. Unfortunately, the friend didn't

20 know a garden hose from an artichoke.

      My father was more disappointed than the rest of us; when he was young, his family use to rise their own produce every summer. He said that if he was to try a garden again, he would plan to spend the entire summer at home.

22

Plurals
and
Possessives

22–1   Forming Plurals (*RHH,* 22a–i)

In the space provided, write the plural form of each word. Consult a dictionary as necessary.

Examples: army   *armies*

        speech   *speeches*

1. traitor   _____

2. warlord   _____

3. son-in-law   _____

4. ghetto   _____

5. baptism   _____

6. bar mitzvah   _____

7. witch _____

8. hero _____

9. Dickens _____

10. cupful _____

11. libretto _____

12. deer _____

13. syllabus _____

14. soprano _____

15. Wilson _____

16. reply _____

17. calf _____

18. child _____

19. datum _____

20. Egg McMuffin _____

22–2 Forming Possessives (*RHH*, 22j–u)

In the space provided, use a possessive noun or pronoun to form a phrase that is equivalent to the phrase on the left.

Examples: the budget of the city   *the city's budget*

poetry written by Yeats   *Yeats's poetry*

the car that belongs to you   *your car*

the property which they own   *their property*

1. poetry written by Miles _____

2. photographs taken by Karsh _____

3. the fragrance it has _____

282

4. the idea conceived by Ms. Koepsel _____

5. the lyrics of Robert Burns _____

6. the speech of the president-elect _____

7. music composed jointly by Lennon
   and McCartney _____

8. music composed by John Lennon
   and by Beethoven _____

9. a night of a hard day _____

10. an orchard that is the joint property
    of Jack and Fern _____

11. the plight of the princess _____

12. the future that belongs to us _____

13. the machinery we own _____

14. the terror of the guillotine _____

15. the reaction of whom _____

16. the typing of Ms. Vasquez _____

17. the circulation of the *New York
    Times* _____

18. the rights of everyone _____

19. the bowling score of Jean Johnson _____

20. the nest in which it lives _____

22–3 Proofreading for Apostrophe Errors
(*RHH,* 22j–u)

The following passages contain errors in the use of apostrophes to show
possession and to indicate omissions. Add apostrophes where necessary and
circle any that are misused.

Example: It's rare these days to find someone who isn't cynical about the job prospects of the class of '88.

PASSAGE 1

In the past month, there have been five robbery's at the local Sac n Pac grocery store. Its little wonder that the owner cant find people to work the night shift. The stores manager finally quit last week after his 57 Chevy was stolen from the parking lot. A week earlier the
5   owner's vicious German shepherd guard dog, Fluffy, lost it's life trying to protect a Wonder Bread delivery man during a hold-up.

PASSAGE 2

My uncle Manley is a true eccentric when it come's to food. He eats all his meals in bed at night—not ordinary meals, but little snacks and pre-packaged treats that he hides in his room during the day. Aunt Pansy claims that she once found nearly fifty Chock Full O Nuts bars under his
5   bed. He's never eaten at restaurants because they serve "tainted" food—"tainted" with what he just does'nt say. His mothers and fathers eating habits were equally eccentric. On her butchers recommendation, his mother ate only mutton. Her husbands preference was for pickled foods—mainly vegetables—which he washed down with large quantities
10   of rye whiskey. Throughout their marriage, they stored food in sep-arate cupboards marked "her's" and his."

PASSAGE 3

Popular sayings among household pet's: "Every dog will have it's day"; "Its a dog-eat-dog world"; "Well, thats a fine kettle of fish"; "Hes an odd fish"; "Shes a rare bird"; "Its raining cat's and dog's"; "Workin like a dog"; "Its a dogs life"; "Dog is mans best
5   friend."

23

Comparing Adjectives and Adverbs

23–1 Eliminating Errors in Comparing Adjectives and Adverbs (*RHH*, 23a–c)

Underline the errors in comparing adjectives and adverbs in the following sentences. Write the correct forms in the space at the end of each sentence. If the sentence contains no error, write C in the space.

Example: The <u>worse</u> thing I saw in the camp was the cheating.   *worst*

1. The room was less darker after Kate had taken down the old rusty screens.   _____

2. "You're getting warmer," said Ryan.   _____

3. Amy will never be thinner than she is now.   _____

4. Nathan preferred a wine somewhat more drier than the Zinfandel Lisa served.   _____

5. That's the less philosophically sound position you've ever taken, said Gil.   _____

6. The contractions came more and more quickly as the car crawled up the hill toward the old hospital.   _____

7. "San Marcos," said Professor Garber, "may be the oldest continually inhabited location on the North American continent."   _____

8. Is Theresa funnier than Aaron?   _____

9. Jeremy felt lower than a snake's belly.   _____

10. They were the most littlest rosebuds Monica had ever seen.   _____

24

Spelling

24-1 Spelling: Words That Look or Sound Alike (*RHH,* 24c)

Examine each pair of words in parentheses and circle the correct one. Use your dictionary or handbook as necessary.

Example: I plan to ((waive), wave) my right ((to), too) a jury trial, even though doing so will adversely ((affect), effect) my chances for an acquittal.

1. Henry is (to, too) tired (to, too) listen to (your, you're) (advice, advise) about (weather, whether) he should go (forward, foreword) with his campaign for governor.

2. If (your, you're) unwilling to (accept, except) the settlement as (its, it's) now defined, (than, then) you should inform the (principal, principle) before you (precede, proceed) with (your, you're) legal challenge.

3. Judge Frolick is not (suppose, supposed) to be (prejudice, prejudiced) (buy, by) such cheap theatrics, but after that last speech, I thought his (bias, biased) was obvious. Yesterday he said the case was (to, too) (miner, minor) for serious attention; now (its, it's) suddenly the most important case he's seen in (some time, sometime).

4. Ann had (all ready, already) written to Paul three times, but her letters seemed to have no (affect, effect) on him. Still, she was determined to (elicit, illicit) some sort of response, so she took out a fountain (pen, pin) and a piece of her best (stationary, stationery) and started a (forth, fourth) letter.

5. (Their, There, They're) were twenty students in the room at 8:00 A.M. waiting for (their, there, they're) test results; at 8:15 the dean entered and announced that eveyone had (passed, past).

6. She (complemented, complimented) several people on the staff (who's, whose) work had deeply (affected, effected) (every one, everyone) in the village.

7. Once the missile left (it's, its) launch (cite, sight, site) in the California (desert, dessert), scientists used a sophisticated tracking (device, devise) (to, too) (altar, alter) (it's, its) (coarse, course).

8. (Everyday, Every day) the (personal, personnel) office processes fifty applications, (every one, everyone) of them from a well-qualified candidate.

9. The (ante-, anti-) nuclear group rented office space on the second floor of a converted (ante-, anti-) bellum home, but (their, there, they're) (presence, presents) didn't seem (to, too) (faze, phase) the other renters, (who's, whose) businesses were on the first floor.

10. (It's, Its) wheels are (loose, lose) and (it's, its) frame is rusty, but the children still ride the old tricycle (every day, everyday).

24–2 Commonly Misspelled Words
(*RHH*, 24d–e)

Circle the misspelled words in the following passages. Then write the correct
spellings in the space above the lines. One of the errors in the first sentence is
corrected for you as an example.

1. He put *a lot* ~~alot~~ of work into his vegtable garden, hopeing to sell part of his
    produce to a locale restaraunt.

2. Although she was only a sophmore, Allison decided to run for president
    of the student goverment. Much to her suprise, her canidacy was en-
    dorsed by one of the campus sororaties.

3. Last Wensday, five atheletes from Taiwan visited the campus for a
    gymnastic exibition. Amoung other things, they preformed a dicsiplined
    series of excercises on the paralell bars, probally one of the finest such
    preformences I've ever seen.

4. The instructer decided to develope a course calander listing the due
    dates for all major assignments. Than she revised her abscence policy,
    making it consistant with the new attendence regulations issued by the
    university during the preceeding semester.

5. We had alot of snow in Febuary, and on several ocassions the temprature
    dropped so low that even vetran Wisconsinites began to complain.

6. Nobody thought that the desparate, starving prisoners had the strenth to
    excape, but through an extrordinary effort, they managed to make it ac-
    cross fourty miles of mountainous terrain, arriving safely at the border
    where they were rescued by local police.

7. His poor judgement, his overly agressive style of managment, his lack
    of disipline, and his tendancy to exagerate his sucesses and ignore his
    failures—all these factors led the firm to a truely disasterous year.

289

Embarassed and outraged, the board of directers fired him as soon as his incredable ineptitude came to light.

8. Michael O'Rear's newest novel is a study in the psycology of terror. By subtley manipulating the reader, he manages to make the villian seem monsterous without making him seem all together unrealistic.

9. During her campaign, the govorner made alot of promises about cleaning up the enviroment, but she now seems unable to fulfill those promises. She still seems knowlegeable about the key issues, but she no longer posesses the committment she once had.

10. Up until last week, things were going alright. Then I had my worst day of the semester: first, I caused a fire in the chemistry labratory; later that day, my English teacher returned a paper marked with twelve mispellings and several errors in grammer; then on Thursday, I had an arguement with my roomate about which of us should controll the thermostat in our room.

24–3 Spelling: Words with *ie* and *ei* Combinations (*RHH*, 24g)

Fill in the blanks with the correct *ie* and *ei* combinations. Use your dictionary or handbook as necessary.

Examples: rec___*ei*___ve

       w___*ei*___rd

1. bel_____ve
2. for_____gn
3. y_____ld
4. c_____ling
5. ach_____ve

6. th_____f
7. fr_____nd
8. s_____ze
9. _____ther
10. spec_____s

11. v_____n	16. effic_____nt
12. w_____gh	17. _____ght
13. pr_____st	18. l_____sure
14. th_____r	19. for_____gn
15. consc_____nce	20. dec_____ve

24–4 Keeping a Spelling List (*RHH*, 24a)

Add to your spelling list the words you missed in the three preceding exercises—24-1, 24-2, and 24-3. As your essays are returned to you, add any misspellings marked by the instructor.

24–5 Using Hyphens (*RHH*, 24i–n)

Insert hyphens as necessary in the following items, and circle hyphens that are not needed. If the item is already correct, write C in the space provided.

Examples: a dog‾eat‾dog world

        a well-mannered child   _C_

        a child that is well mannered   _C_

1. a well-guarded secret   _____

2. a secret that is well-guarded   _____

3. the well to do banker   _____

4. a building that is seventy five years old   _____

5. a fifty-five-year-old house   _____

6. a convincingly-argued proposal   _____

7. my ex professor   _____

8. mayor-elect Farr   _____

9. the exam has three parts   _____

10. a three part exam   _____

11. a hotter than usual summer _____

12. right-to-work law _____

13. a pro-Fascist organization _____

14. her stunningly brilliant mind _____

15. a price cut by one-half _____

16. un American activities _____

17. McCarthy like tactics _____

18. tactics similar to those that McCarthy-used _____

25

Capitals

25–1 Using Capitalization (*RHH,* 25a–t)

The following passage contains numerous errors in capitalization. Circle any letters that *should* be capitalized, and strike through any that are capitalized unnecessarily. The first few errors have been corrected for you as an example.

Kate O'Flaherty was born in St. Louis in 1851. Her Father was a successful st. louis merchant who had married into an Aristocratic family of french origin. Kate attended the best school available to young women in the City; then spent two years busy with the social activities appropriate to a person of her class; in 1870 she married oscar chopin, of a prominent Louisiana creole family, and moved with him to new orleans.

In the twelve years of their marriage, she bore him six children; and upon his sudden death in the early 1880s, she assumed the management of the Family Plantation in natchitoches, Louisiana. In 1884 she returned to her Mother's home in st.

louis, and only after her Mother's death the next year did she begin serious writing. Her first Novel, *at fault,* appeared in 1890 and was followed by two collections of Short Stories, *Bayou folk* in 1894 and *A Night In Acadia* in 1897. By the time *the awakening* appeared in 1899, she was the well-known author of over a hundred Stories, Sketches, and Essays which had appeared in the popular and Literary Magazines of the period. She died in 1904.

Published in 1899 by herbert s. stone (chicago), *the awakening* met with widespread hostile criticism, and the book was removed from the Library shelves in st. louis. Chopin herself was refused membership in the st. louis fine arts club because of the novel. In 1906 it was reprinted by duffield (new york); but then it went out of print and remained so for more than half a Century in this Country.[2]

Note: For more information on the controversy surrounding Chopin's novel, see the book cited in the note for the above passage.

26

Italics,
Abbreviations,
Numbers

26–1 Eliminating Errors in the Use of Italics, Abbreviations, and Numbers (*RHH*, 26a–n)

Using your handbook as a reference tool, edit the following sentences. First underline words and phrases that should be italicized. Then cross out errors in the use of abbreviations and numbers and make corrections in the space above the lines. (Assume that the sentences in this exercise come from nontechnical prose—a college essay of the sort you would submit in your writing course.)

Example: <u>Bilker's Digest</u> ran a story last week about ~~2~~ *two* brothers from Punta

Gorda, ~~Fl.~~ *Florida*, who made ~~twenty-six thousand dollars~~ *#26,000* in a single

day; they managed to sell nearly a hundred people on a bogus

Caribbean cruise aboard the <u>Love Boat II</u>.

1. Most of Herman Melville's novel Moby-Dick takes place at sea, aboard
   the Pequod.

2. Mr. Wacker, the new football coach, warned the team: "Before this training session is over, you will all know the meaning of the word pain."

3. Aeschylus, the great Greek tragedian, probably wrote nearly 90 plays, including Prometheus Bound; he lived from 525–456 B.C.

4. In late Oct., Prof. Clifton D. Rodar, D.D.S., will give a lecture entitled, "Your Future in Dental School." Currently on leave from the Martindale College of Dentistry, Dr. Rodar is author of the best-selling book, You and Your Teeth.

5. Asked to name 5 books of the Bible, Tiffany could name only three— Genesis, Job, and Ruth.

6. The house at 211 Harvard sold for an astounding two-hundred and twenty-eight thousand dollars.

7. Honi soit qui mal y pense is the motto of the Order of the Garter.

8. Greta finally won the Scrabble game by using the word flocculus on a triple word score.

9. The U.S. Olympic team won 17 gold medals, thirty-six silver medals, and 14 bronze medals.

10. The CIA and FBI were notified about the incursion at 2:00 A.M. on the morning of Feb. 3rd.

26–2 Review Exercise: Editing a Passage for Errors in Plurals, Possessives, Spelling, Capitals, Italics, Abbreviations, Numbers, and Hyphens (*RHH,* 22a–u, 24a–n, 25a–t, 26a–n)

Carefully proofread the following passages for misspellings and for errors in the use of plurals, possessives, capitals, italics, abbreviations, numbers, and hyphens. First, underline words and phrases that should be italicized. Then cross out the other errors, and make corrections in the space above the lines. The first two sentences are done for you as an example.[3]

PASSAGE 1

Peter Weir is perhaps the ^A̶australian ^d̶irector who is most famous abroad. His Picnic At Hanging ^Rrock (1975) became the first Australian film to ~~attrack~~ *attract* ^iInternational attention. His Gallipoli, released through paramount, and The year Of Living Dangerously, to be released by mgm, were amoung the first australian films to hook up with Hollywood for mass release worldwide.

Weir comes from a University background of Arts and Law. He began to shoot 16-mm. underground movies while makeing a living doing odd jobs in london and was then hired to make documentarys. Now thirty-eight, he lives with his wife and children at palm beach, a geographically superier version of malibu, about 50 miles North of sydney.

PASSAGE 2

Australias least pretintious but most financially rewarded directer is George Miller, who's Mad Max (1979) and this years The Road Warrier are International blockbusters, earning more money then any other australian film. The hero of both films is a loner named max, who is more or less coerced into standing up to a viscious gang of motorcycle riding thugs who are plagueing some oil refinery people in post holocaust Australia.

A chubby, twinkly eyed gamin of thirty-six, Miller gloats, "I make B pictures." He grew up in rural queensland and went on to enter Medical School. In his last year there, he helped his twin brother make a 1 min. film. This led to a month long University course in film making, than some shorts depicting Millers cinematic preoccupation with the sinistor and the violant. For a while, Miller was a practicing medical doctor, making house calls to finance his entry into cinima.

27

Forming and Spacing Punctuation Marks

27–1 Forming and Spacing Punctuation Marks with a Typewriter (*RHH*, 27a–k)

In each of the following pairs, identify the sentence that violates the conventions for punctuating with a typewriter. Circle each error.

Example: (a) In two months⊙the hottest of the year, I admit⊙we

spent over $400.00 for air conditioning.

(b) In two months--the hottest of the year, I admit--we

spent over $400.00 for air conditioning.

1. (a) Earl Warren served as Chief Justice of the United States

(1953 - 1969) and as governor of California (1943 - 1953).

(b) Earl Warren served as Chief Justice of the United States

(1953-1969) and as governor of California (1943-1953).

2. (a) Some people considered the course a challenge; others thought it was merely impossible.

   (b) Some people considered the course a challenge; others thought it was merely impossible.

3. (a) The professor said that her course would strengthen the ill-prepared---if they could survive the first test.

   (b) The professor said that her course would strengthen the ill-prepared--if they could survive the first test.

4. (a) Several of T.S. Eliot's poems--would he have imagined it possible--, have been set to music for the Broadway musical Cats.

   (b) Several of T. S. Eliot's poems--would he have imagined it possible--have been set to music for the Broadway musical Cats.

5. (a) The columnist argued that the country "would be better served by a single-term, six-year presidency...than by the present system allowing two four-year terms."

   (b) The columnist argued that the country "would be better served by a single-term, six-year presidency . . . than by the present system allowing two four-year terms."

VII
THE
RESEARCH ESSAY

28

Finding and Mastering Sources

28–1 Acquainting Yourself with a Research Library (*RHH*, 28a–c)

Visit the library in which you plan to do your research. Then complete the following exercise.[1]

1. What are the library's hours? _____

2. For how long can a book be checked out? _____

3. What is the library's policy on renewals? _____

   _____

   _____

4. Can you recall a book from another reader if you need it immediately?

   _____

   What is the procedure for doing so? _____

_____

_____

5. Where is the library's card catalog located? _____

_____

Use it to find the title and call number of a book on each of the following topics:

A. World War II _____

_____

B. The Egyptian pyramids _____

_____

C. Clothing of the 1920s _____

_____

D. Farming methods _____

_____

E. Edgar Allan Poe _____

_____

6. Does the library have an interlibrary loan service? _____
If so, what is the procedure for using it? _____

_____

_____

_____

7. Is there a special section for reserve books? _____ If so, list
the title and call number of one book that is currently on reserve.

_____

8. Where is the reference room (or desk) located? _____

_____

9. Where is the *New York Times Index* located? _____

   _____

   What color is the cover of the most recent volume?_____

10. Where is the *Readers' Guide to Periodical Literature* located?

    _____

    What color is the cover of the most recent volume?_____

11. Where is the *Book Review Digest* located? _____

    _____

    What color is the cover of the most recent volume?_____

12. Does the library have a collection of microfilm and microfiche? _____
    If so, give the title and call number of a newspaper stored on microfilm.

    _____

    _____

    What is the headline story on the front page of this newspaper for the
    day you were born? _____

    _____

13. Where are the current periodicals located? _____

    _____

    How are they organized? _____

    _____

    _____

14. What is the procedure for locating a periodical published before 1975?

    _____

    _____

    _____

    _____

15. Where are the current newspapers located? _____

_____

How are they organized? _____

_____

28-2 Using Background Sources for a Broad Introduction to a Subject (*RHH*, 28d)

Give the title of a reference source (other than a general encyclopedia) in which you could find a broad introduction to each of the following subjects. Look up one of the subjects, and briefly explain the type of information you found.

1. Ludwig van Beethoven _____

   _____

2. The writings of Sigmund Freud _____

   _____

3. The New York Stock Exchange _____

   _____

4. Science fiction_____

   _____

5. Major religions in the United States or Canada _____

   _____

6. Type of information found in *one* of the five sources

   _____

   _____

   _____

   _____

   _____

   _____

28–3 Using Background Sources to Locate Specific Information (*RHH*, 28d)

For each field listed below, locate a reference source other than a general encyclopedia. Then, in the space provided, write the title of the source and a *specific* item of information that you found in it.

Example: Music *American Popular Music: A Reference Guide / The first stereo long-playing records were marketed in the U. S. in 1958.*

1. Education _____

2. Literature _____

3. Business_____

4. Psychology_____

5. Science/technology _____

28–4 Taking Notes from Your Reading (*RHH*, 28e)

Assume that you are gathering source material for a research paper about the recent teacher shortage in the United States. You plan to emphasize the *causes for the shortage.* With that topic in mind, study the following passages. Then write two note cards for each passage, using the models given in *The Random House Handbook,* pp. 495–496.

1. a bibliography card containing the information given at the end of the passage
2. a content card containing a quotation from the passage along with a brief comment noting why the quotation is relevant to the topic (causes for the teacher shortage)

PASSAGE A

Still, teachers' hours remain long (at least for the conscientious), working conditions are often poor, and the pay is terrible. While the average teacher's salary is just over $20,000, that figure reflects the pay of a corps of veterans. The average salary for beginning teachers with a B.A. is $12,769, about $4,200 less than a fledgling accountant can make. Even worse, after 15 years the accountant will be making between $40,000 and $50,000, while the teacher will be earning less than $25,000. A Carnegie Foundation report last month concluded that teachers' salaries declined 12.2% between 1972 and 1982, when inflation was factored in, while total personal income increased by 17.8% in real dollars during the same period. Reason enough for sporadic strikes. Chicago teachers, for instance, may go out this week.

[Source: An article, "The Bold Quest for Quality," by Ellie McGrath, appearing in the October 10, 1983, issue of *Time,* pages 58–66. This passage appears on page 63.]

PASSAGE A: BIBLIOGRAPHY CARD

PASSAGE A: CONTENT CARD

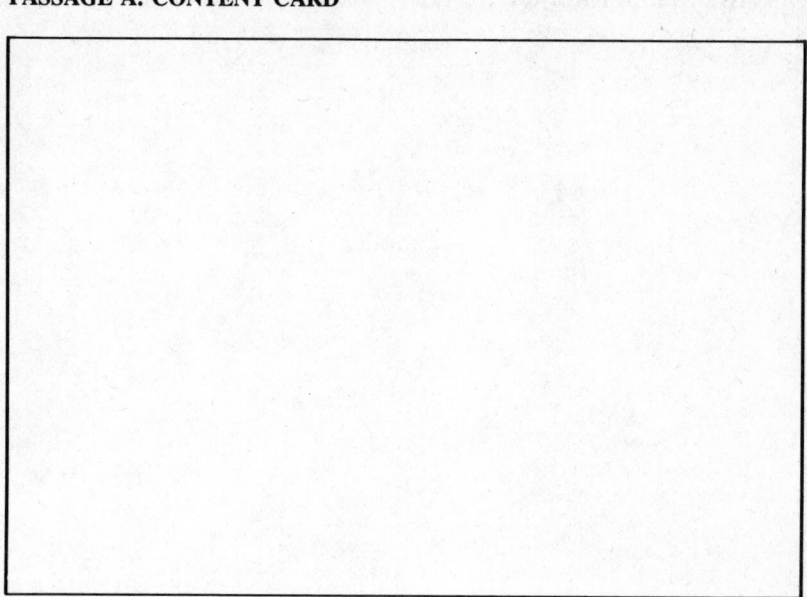

PASSAGE B

In countries where the intellectual functions of education are highly valued, like France and Germany and the Scandinavian countries, the teacher, especially the secondary-school teacher, is likely to be an important local figure representing a personal and vocational ideal worthy of emulation. There it seems worth becoming a teacher because what the teacher does is worth doing and is handsomely recognized. The intellectually alert and cultivated teacher may have a particular importance for intelligent children whose home environment is not highly cultivated; such children have no alternative course of mental stimulation. All too often, however, in the history of the United States, the schoolteacher has been in no position to serve as a model for an introduction to the intellectual life. Too often he has not only no claims to an intellectual life of his own, but not even an adequate workmanlike competence in the skills he is supposed to impart. Regardless of his own quality, his low pay and common lack of personal freedom have caused the teacher's role to be associated with exploitation and intimidation.

[Source: A book called *Anti-Intellectualism in American Life,* written by historian Richard Hofstadter. The book was published in 1963 by Alfred A. Knopf, New York. The passage appears on page 310.]

PASSAGE B: BIBLIOGRAPHY CARD

PASSAGE B: CONTENT CARD

28–5 Summarizing and Paraphrasing
Source Material (*RHH,* 28f)

On your own paper write a summary and a paraphrase, using the source material given in the preceding exercise (28–4).

1. Write a *summary* of passage A. Use your own words to state the author's main ideas as concisely and accurately as possible.
2. Write a *paraphrase* of passage B. Closely follow the order of the passage and include main points along with important supporting details. Take care, however, not to repeat the author's wording unless you use quotation marks.

29

Documenting
Sources

29–1   Avoiding Plagiarism: Quoting and Paraphrasing (*RHH*, 29a)

Write a paragraph in which you use at least two quotations from the source material given in Exercise 28–4. Introduce the material you borrow, and use quotation marks as necessary. If you paraphrase either source or rely directly on the authors' facts and ideas, underline those parts of your paragraph (besides the quotations) that should be acknowledged by a citation. Use your own paper.

29–2   Recognizing Plagiarism (*RHH*, 29a)

Read the following passages. The writer of passage B has quoted and paraphrased material from passage A. Put quotation marks around any direct borrowings, and underline any paraphrased material that the writer should acknowledge.

PASSAGE A: THE SOURCE

> What happens if you smoke during pregnancy? Briefly, smoking during pregnancy stunts the baby's growth and possibly diminishes its

IQ; it increases the risk of miscarriage; it can cause serious complications in pregnancy and delivery, such as placental separation,
5 which can be fatal; and it increases the chances of a child's dying just before or after birth. These are the disturbing reports from two decades of studies conducted in many countries throughout the world. One of the largest and most thorough investigations, the United States Collaborative Perinatal Project, examined more than five
10 thousand pregnancies at twelve major hospital centers in the United States and concluded that smoking during pregnancy produces a long list of risks to the unborn and newborn child. Researchers in the study noted an increased risk of fetal death or damage, a delay in fetal growth, and an increased likelihood of pregnancy-related com-
15 plications for the mother.[2]

PASSAGE B: THE WRITER'S PARAGRAPH

Women today are more aware than they were a few years ago of the importance of prenatal care for their babies. Until recently, the unborn child was thought to absorb from the mother only the nutrients needed for proper growth. Scientists now know that whatever
5 the mother takes into her body—food, drink, drugs, cigarette smoke —is likely to have a direct effect for good or for bad upon the health of the fetus. Smoking during pregnancy, for example, stunts the baby's growth and possibly diminishes IQ. Most people assume that a smoker would give up her habit during pregnancy once she learned
10 these facts, facts that are confirmed by two decades of studies conducted in many countries throughout the world. Yet many well-informed women do continue to smoke during pregnancy, even when faced with evidence such as that gathered recently by U.S. scientists who studied thousands of pregnancies at a dozen hospitals.
15 These scientists discovered that smoking mothers take great risks: a high rate of fetal death or damage, retarded growth of the fetus, and a greater chance of complications for themselves during pregnancy.

29–3 Using a Reference List: MLA Style (*RHH,* 29c)

For each of the following items, write a reference list entry using the appropriate MLA style. Then arrange the entries alphabetically. Use your own paper.

1. A quotation from page 91 of *Word Processing on the KayPro,* a book by Peter A. McWilliams. The quotation is from the first edition, published in July 1983 by Prelude Press of Los Angeles, California.

2. A quotation from page 41 of the sixth edition of R. R. Palmer and Joel Colton's book, *A History of the Modern World.* The book lists six copyright dates: 1950, 1956, 1965, 1970, 1977, and 1983. It was published by Alfred A. Knopf, Inc., of New York, New York.

3. A reference to *The Chicago Manual of Style.* No author or editor is listed. The book, in its thirteenth edition, was published by the University of Chicago Press in 1982. The title page lists the location of the press as Chicago and London.

4. A quotation from page 200 through 201 of "Jewish Writers," an essay by Mark Shechner. The essay appears on pages 191 through 239 of the *Harvard Guide to Contemporary American Writing,* a book edited by Daniel Hoffman. The book was published in 1979 by the Harvard University Press. The title page lists the location of the press as Cambridge, Massachusetts, and London, England.

5. A quotation from page 433 of "Anthony Powell, Nicolas Poussin, and the Structure of Time," an article by Henry R. Harrington, which appears on pages 431 through 448 of the Winter 1983 issue of *Contemporary Literature.* The issue is also labeled Volume 24, Number 3. The journal uses continuous pagination through each year's volume.

6. A reference to "Some Reluctant Friends," an article by Pico Iyer, which appears on pages 38 through 40 of the July 16, 1984, issue of *Time* magazine. The issue is also labeled Volume 123, Number 3. Each issue of *Time* has separate pagination.

7. A quotation from "Stellar Physics," a book review on page 1139 of *Science* magazine, June 5, 1981, Volume 212, Number 4499. The reviewer is Sidney C. Wolff; the book reviewed is *The Brightest Star,* by Cornelis De Jager.

8. A reference to "Iraq Takes Lukewarm Approach to Hot War," an article by Ned Temko in *The Christian Science Monitor,* a daily newspaper. The article begins on page 1 and is continued and concluded on page 32 of the July 9, 1984 issue.

9. An unsigned newspaper editorial, "Hunter Safety," in the *Austin-American Statesman*. The editorial appears on page 2, Section C, of the July 8, 1984, issue.

10. "Coffee," an entry by William C. Struning in the 1976 edition of *Encyclopedia Americana*.

29–4 Using a Reference List: APA Style
(*RHH*, 29c)

For each item in Exercise 29-3, write a reference list entry using APA style. Then arrange the entries alphabetically. Use your own paper.

29–5 Using Endnotes (*RHH*, 29e)

For each item in Exercise 29-3, write an endnote using the "alternative MLA" style. Arrange the items consecutively on an endnote page. Use your own paper.

30

Planning and Writing a Research Essay

30–1 Arriving at a Trial Topic

Select a subject area from the following list. Then, working alone or with a group of classmates, write down five topics for a brief research paper. State each topic in the form of a question. In arriving at the topics, use whatever pre-writing method you wish—reviewing your experiences and reading, free-writing, brainstorming, asking questions.

Example: Subject: Pollution

Topics: How has smog affected Los Angeles in the past twenty years?

Are the Great Lakes more or less polluted today than they were in the 1960s?

What are the effects of acid rain on the environment?

Is noise pollution a serious problem or merely an annoyance?

Who should pay for the clean-up of toxic waste dumps—government or industry?

Advertising   Minorities
Censorship   Music
Computers   Nutrition
Cults   Prisons/Punishment
Education   Sports/Athletics
Fads   The Women's Movement
Medicine/Health Care   Violence
Marriage

Subject: _____

Topic questions:

1. _____
   _____
   _____

2. _____
   _____
   _____

3. _____
   _____
   _____

4. _____
   _____
   _____

5. _____
   _____
   _____

30–2 Testing a Trial Topic

Test the five topics you developed for the preceding exercise by answering the
following questions:

1. *Interest:* Is the topic interesting and significant enough to justify the writer's time in conducting research and the instructor's time in reading the results of the research?

2. *Limitation:* Is the topic too broad and complex to cover adequately in a brief research paper, or is it too narrow and simple for a paper of the assigned length?

3. *Sources:* Is the writer likely to find enough research material to support a paper on this topic? What types of sources are likely to be most useful?

30–3 Exploring a Trial Topic

Select one of the topics you tested in the preceding exercise (30–2), and jot down some preliminary questions that it raises. Does any question suggest a way to narrow the topic further, to move toward a possible thesis? Which questions are most likely to lead to fruitful research?

Example: Topic: What are the effects of acid raid on the environment?

Exploratory questions: What exactly is acid rain? What causes it? Does everyone agree on the cause? Is the rain harmful to animals and plants? To people? Is there any way to prevent acid rain? Why are the Canadians (according to many newspaper reports) so concerned about acid rain?

Topic: _____

Exploratory questions:

_____

_____

_____

_____

_____

_____

_____

_____

30–4 Evaluating Proposals for Research Essays

Evaluate the following proposals for seven- to ten-page research essays. Which of the four looks most promising? What advice would you give the students as they modify their topics or formulate new ones? Write your comments in the space provided.

PROPOSAL 1

I plan to study the use of vitamin supplements in the North American diet. First, I will describe the history of vitamin supplements, explaining when and why they developed and how they became popular. Second, I will describe how vitamins are made and what kinds of chemicals they contain. In the third part of the paper, I will discuss whether vitamin supplements are really necessary in the North American diet. I expect this to be the longest part of the paper. Judging from my preliminary reading, I will take the position that most vitamin supplements are unnecessary. In the final part of the paper, I will argue that misleading advertising by drug companies is responsible for the use of millions of unnecessary vitamins.

PROPOSAL 2

Was Lyndon B. Johnson a good President? I will attempt in my paper to answer this question by looking at both sides of the issue. First, I will present evidence showing that Johnson was an unsuccessful President. Then I will present the case of those who say that he was effective. In the final part of the paper, I will evaluate the two sides and present my conclusion that Johnson was a good President despite the many criticisms made against him.

PROPOSAL 3

Because of my interest in dentistry as a profession, I intend to write a paper on the job-related stress experienced by dentists. In my preliminary reading, I found that dentists do experience a great deal of stress because of the way they are perceived by patients (painful, not healing) and because of the intense concentration, confined working areas, and high-pitched noises associated with their jobs. One source said that job stress may partly explain the unusually high rate of suicide among dentists. I plan to divide my paper into three main sections. First, I will explain the concept of job stress—its symptoms and its effects. Second, I will describe the reasons for the high levels of stress experienced by dentists. Finally, I will discuss the effects of this stress.

_____

_____

_____

_____

_____

PROPOSAL 4

My paper will describe the process used to make home-brewed beer. Drawing from my own experience and from three books on the subject, I will first describe the various types of beer that can be made at home. This will take about one-third of the paper. In the rest of the paper, I will give step-by-step instructions for making beer and ale. This part of the paper will be organized around the five main steps in the beer-making process.

_____

_____

_____

_____

_____

30–5 Evaluating Research Paper Outlines and Introductions

Compare the following student outlines and introductory paragraphs for seven- to ten-page research papers. The assigned general topic was "Early

Developments in the Computer Industry.'' Which outline and introduction look more promising? Why? If the writers were submitting this work for your consideration *before* they continued to write their first drafts, what advice would you give them? Use the space provided to summarize your comments.

PAPER 1

Title: Early Computers

Tentative Thesis: The main computers which started the age of data processing were the ENIAC, EDVAC, UNIVAC, and Whirlwind.

Outline:

   I. Introduction

  II. ENIAC

 III. EDVAC

 IV. UNIVAC

  V. Whirlwind

 VI. Conclusion

Introduction:

    The invention of the computer in the late 1940s and early 1950s provided people with the ability to do large calculations in a matter of seconds. The first electronic digital computer was invented in 1946. After its invention, many people did not realize the potential ability of computers. In the brief time we have had computers, the rate of growth of this industry has changed greatly. This growth began in the early 1950s when computers were made for sale. The most important and well-known early computers were the ENIAC, EDVAC, UNIVAC I, and Whirlwind I. Each of these computers has a different importance in the history of computers, and each will be discussed separately.*

_____

_____

_____

_____

_____

PAPER 2

Title: Major Advances in the Computer Industry, 1950–1955

Tentative Thesis: From 1950 to 1955, computer hardware became smaller and faster than it had been before, making possible the efficient handling of scientific information and the application of the computer to growing business needs.

Outline:

I. Background and Thesis

II. Developments in 1950

   A. REAC

   B. IBM Model 701

   C. Whirlwind I

   D. SEAC

III. Developments in 1951--Improved Memory

   A. UNIVAC

   B. Electrostatic Memory

IV. Developments from 1952 to 1954--Mainly in Software

V. Developments in 1955--Shift Back to Hardware

   A. TRANSAC

   B. IBM Model 702

   C. IBM Model 608

   D. Input/Output Devices

VI. Summary of Benefits

   A. Aircraft Industry

   B. Military

   C. Business

Introduction:

One of these days all of us may be walking around with tiny computers on our wrists, or we may at least have computers in our homes. Even today the computer is playing a major role in our lives. Its importance can be attributed partially to the advances that were made in the industry between 1950 and 1955. During this period, much of the hardware that was developed became smaller and faster than it had been before, making possible the efficient handling of scientific information and the application of the computer to growing business needs.*

_____

_____

_____

_____

_____

30–6 Analyzing a Completed Research Paper

Working alone or with a group of classmates, study the student research essay reprinted here. Then complete the exercise that follows it.

Diana Hall
English 1320
Ms. McElyea
15 April 1984

When It Rains It Pours

In recent years, Americans have become increasingly aware of the many pollutants damaging their environment. One of the most controversial of these is acid rain--rain which contains an abnormally high level of sulfates and nitrates (Tver). These acidic chemicals are released into the air from power plants and other sources. Once in the atmosphere, they mix with the moisture in the clouds and are carried hundreds of miles by the wind, eventually drifting down to earth in the form of rain, snow, or fog. One Canadian government publication, Fact Sheet on Acid Rain, points out that rain "ten or more times as acidic as normal has been occurring frequently in the northeastern U.S. and Canada." This rain is a dangerous pollutant that continues to damage the environment and to strain political relations between the United States and Canada.

Acid rain is slowly destroying the ecosystems of many lakes in the northeastern United States and Canada. A lake's ecosystem is made up of many different plants and animals that work together to support one another. John T. Baccus, a biology professor at Southwest Texas State University, explains that when acid rain falls into these lakes, the acid level is increased beyond the tolerance of the organisms living there. David Tver reports that many lakes are already badly affected:

> According to Science News, February 2, 1979, the Adirondack lakes were becoming fishless because of acid rain and a 1978-79 survey of 85 lakes in the Boundary Waters Canoe Area along the Minnesota-Ontario border showed that two-thirds of them were near the brink of acidity where fish-life could not be supported.

Once acid rain destroys an ecosystem, that system cannot be put back into its original form. According to Professor Baccus, we do not have enough scientific knowledge to restore an ecosystem that has taken thousands of years to evolve.

Acid rain not only presents a major problem for the ecosystems found in lakes, but also creates difficulties for plant-life and the soils in which they grow. Joseph A. Davis explains that the alkaline soils found in the upper regions of the United States and the lower eastern regions of Canada have a natural buffering capacity which can neutralize the acid up to a certain point ("Acid Rain Still a Sore Point" 1063). However, these soils cannot buffer the large amount of acid rain that falls on them. According to Robert Ostmann, author of Acid Rain: A Plague Upon the Waters,

> many scientists believe that continuing or worsening acid deposition could reduce the productivity of vital forests and farmlands, disrupt the crucial, life-sustaining process of plant photosynthesis in large areas, and poison some drinking water supplies and food fish stocks (13).

Professor Jack Corbett, a political scientist at Southwest Texas State University, points out that acid rain not only disrupts plant photosynthesis, but also hinders plant growth; Corbett explains that when acid rain falls on a plant's new buds, it can kill the buds, thwarting growth almost before it begins (personal interview).

The serious consequences of acid rain are clear, but its causes are less apparent. Some acid rain comes from natural sources, such as volcanic eruptions and plant photosynthesis (Tver). However, scientists believe that much acid rain is caused by the burning of coal with a high sulfur content. Robert Ostmann supports this theory, stating that "in one year the sulfur-dioxide emissions from a large coalfired plant can equal the high amount released by the May 18, 1980, eruption of Mount St. Helens" (11). And according to a report from the National Academy of Sciences, there is "overwhelming" circumstantial evidence linking acid rain to power plant emissions (Fact Sheet).

Many people, however, still dispute the theory that most acid rain is caused by the burning of high-sulfur coal. They argue that not enough evidence exists to prove the actual causes of acid rain and that scientists should not single out power plants. Once again, these people are proven wrong by Joseph A. Davis, who confirms that "the region emitting the most sulfur dioxide is the Ohio River Valley, where states like Ohio, Indiana, and Kentucky burn large amounts of high-sulfur coal" ("No Reagan Acid Rain Legislation" 2187). This high-sulfur coal is used to produce electrical energy and also to provide jobs for thousands of Americans.

While most scientists agree that acid rain is caused by the burning of high-sulfur coal, the United States government has claimed repeatedly that there is insufficient evidence to establish the sources of acid rain, a claim that has caused serious political friction between the United States and Canada. Joseph Davis sums up the situation, stating that "acid rain is literally eating away the sandstone of Canada's Parliament buildings and showering diplomatic fallout on the U. S. Capital" ("Acid Rain Still a Sore Point" 1063).

Many Canadians believe that the United States is responsible for most acidic air pollution that falls in their country. Jack Corbett tends to agree with them. While admitting that it is difficult to determine which specific damage in Canada is done by which source, Corbett claims that more acid rain is produced in the United States than in Canada (personal interview). Canadians are frustrated at the United States for not acting promptly on what they consider an important environmental issue. Corbett explains that the Canadians' sense of urgency and frustration appears to be "matched by a general U. S. reluctance to do anything beyond a moderate amount of research and release of press statements attesting to its continuing interest" ("Acid Rain"). The United States' general reluctance seems to be the main cause of strained political ties between the two traditionally friendly countries.

Although the United States and Canada's political ties are strained, there is a continuing effort to make progress on the issue of acid rain. Several major scientific panels in the United States have studied the problem, including the National Research Council and the National Acid Precipitation Task Force (Davis, "No Reagan Acid Rain Legislation" 2187). The Canadian Embassy's Fact Sheet on Acid Rain lists many of the findings of these and other groups, findings that provide a basis for discussion between the two countries. Since 1976 Canada and the United States have conducted a series of formal and informal talks about acid rain; however, these talks have not led to dramatic progress. For example, in 1982 Canada proposed a plan in which each nation would reduce industrial emissions by 25 percent. After negotiations, the United States rejected the proposal because, as one newspaper put it, "not enough is known about acid rain to justify the huge expense of Canada's proposal" ("As Lakes Quietly Die").

Cost estimates, however, vary greatly depending on the source. Corbett explains that "research data on economic costs are somewhat sparse, and are frequently generated by those with a vested interest in a particular outcome" ("Acid Rain"). If utility companies have to pay for clean-up costs, it would mean higher electric rates for consumers. And many people might have to pay with their jobs if companies decide to move elsewhere rather than pay the high cost of emission control. Corbett says that the United Mine Workers estimate that the most restrictive legislation to control acid rain would cost up to 89,000 jobs in coal mining in the Midwest and South (personal interview).

Although lost jobs and increased utility rates are important, one must also consider other losses that Americans and Canadians may face if the acid rain problem is not controlled in the near future: the loss of animal and plant life in the lakes of both countries.

There are ways in which the United States could control acid rain and improve its relations with Canada. Davis suggests that "one of the cheaper ways to reduce sulfur dioxide is to burn low-sulfur Western coal" ("No Reagan Acid Rain Legislation"). The burning of low-sulfur coal would be effective, but better legislation would also help. Currently, older power plants are not required to have the same emission-control standards as the newer plants. In fact, the older plants, according to Davis, are "allowed higher emissions for years or decades until they are retired" ("Acid Rain Still a Sore Point"). If a new law were passed ordering all power plants to have stringent emissions controls, then the amount of acid rain falling on the United States and Canada could be reduced considerably. Acid rain could also be controlled more efficiently if the Reagan administration showed more concern about the acid rain issue. Robert Ostmann describes the administration's policy as one of "growth, expansion, using more energy and more resources to become powerful--these are the nation's priorities, not environmental integrity" (184).

Although growth and expansion are important for our economy, the protection of the environment should also be a high priority. If acid rain is not reduced considerably, the United States and Canada may witness serious damage to their environment. This damage already threatens some of our valuable natural resources and may someday disrupt our environment seriously enough to affect our food supply. If the government takes action now, it can slow the irreversible damage of acid rain and ease the current strain on our relations with Canada.

Works Cited

"As Lakes Quietly Die, the U. S. and Canada Feud Over Acid Rain," Washington Post 27 Sept. 1982, sec. 1: 1.

Baccus, John T. Personal interview. 2 Mar. 1984.

Corbett, Jack. "Acid Rain in Canadian-United States Relations: The Politics of Inaction," Canadian Political Science Association Annual Meeting. Vancouver, BC, 6-8 June 1983.

---. Personal interview. 2 Mar. 1984.

Davis, Joseph A. "Acid Rain Still a Sore Point for United States, Canada: But Both Sides Are Optimistic," Congressional Quarterly 28 May 1983: 1063-1065.

---. "No Reagan Acid Rain Legislation in Sight," Congressional Quarterly 22 Oct. 1983: 2186-2187.

Fact Sheet on Acid Rain, Washington, DC: Canadian Embassy, n.d.

Ostmann, Robert, Jr. Acid Rain: A Plague Upon the Waters. Minneapolis: Dillon P, 1982.

Tver, David F. "Acid Precipitation," Dictionary of Dangerous Pollutants, Ecology, and Environment. New York: Industrial P, 1981.

STUDY QUESTIONS FOR "WHEN IT RAINS IT POURS"

1. Identify the writer's thesis. Is the topic of the essay adequately limited for a brief research essay? Explain.

2. Is the first paragraph an effective introduction? Explain.

3. Is the essay well organized? Point out specific examples to illustrate your answer. Then write a subordinated outline showing the main points developed in the essay.

4. Does the writer clearly explain the causes and effects of acid rain? Should any point be explained more fully?

5. The writer acknowledges that there is disagreement about the causes of acid rain. Does she give adequate consideration to those who disagree with her explanation of the causes of acid rain? Explain.

6. In discussing the U.S.-Canadian conflict over acid rain, does the author seem fair to both sides? Explain, pointing out specific examples.

7. Is the writer's conclusion effective? Why or why not?

8. Evaluate the writer's use of sources. Specifically, make a list of the different types of sources used. Do the number and variety of sources seem appropriate? What advantages does the writer gain by using personal interviews with two of her professors? What, if any, are the disadvantages of using such interviews?

9. Summarize your evaluation of the essay by listing its major strengths and weaknesses.

10. What advice would you give the writer if she were revising the essay? Be specific.

30–7 Using a Checklist to Plan Your Research Paper

Use the following checklist as a guide for planning your paper. Your instructor may want to collect some of your work as you move through the various stages on the list; if so, indicate due dates in the left margin. Remember that the checklist is a general guide, not a detailed program for completing the essay. Be prepared to be flexible. For example, you may have to modify your thesis at any point in the project, or you may find yourself returning to the library for further research even as you draft the essay.

1. *Select a topic.* If your instructor suggests a general subject area, narrow it until you find a trial topic that interests you and falls within the limits of the assignment.

2. *Get an overview of the topic.* Formulate several questions about the topic and do some preliminary reading to see which questions look most promising. Take notes.

3. *Prepare a working bibliography.* List the books, articles, and other sources that appear to be most significant for the topic. Continue reading and taking notes.

4. *Formulate a trial thesis.* Based on your early reading and thinking about the topic, formulate a trial thesis and, if possible, a tentative outline.

5. *Take detailed notes.* With your trial thesis in mind, take detailed notes from the sources you have gathered. Be prepared to follow any new leads suggested by your research.

6. *Revise your thesis and outline.* Revise your thesis and outline to match the evidence you have gathered.

7. *Write a first draft.* Using your revised thesis and outline to guide you, write a first draft of the essay. Keep track of sources as you write, making notes in the margins to indicate where you quote or paraphrase the work of others.

8. *Revise.* If possible, get reactions to your draft. Acting on the suggestions of others and on your own careful evaluation of the paper, make any necessary conceptual, organizational, and editorial changes. Plan your revision using the Checklist for Revision in *The Random House Handbook,* pp. 120–121.

9. *Prepare your reference list.* Double check all citations in the essay; then prepare your reference list, making sure that it includes all sources that you use in your paper. (*Note:* If your instructor prefers endnotes and a bibliography, prepare them using the appropriate forms.)

10. *Prepare the final copy.* Following the manuscript conventions given in the handbook, type or handwrite the final copy of your essay. Proofread carefully before submitting.

Notes

PART I

1. Sigurd Olson, *Of Time and Place* (New York: Knopf, 1982) 69.
2. Joyce Carey, *The Horse's Mouth* (London: Michael Joseph, 1951) 11.
3. Charles H. Miller, *Auden: An American Friendship* (New York: Scribner's, 1983) 100–101.
4. D. H. Lawrence, *The Rainbow* (New York: Penguin, 1981) 49.
5. Frances Fitzgerald, *Cities on a Hill: A Journey through Contemporary American Cultures* (New York: Simon & Schuster, 1986) 203–204.
6. W. Thomas Jones and Betsy Bush, "A Mound of One's Own," *Natural History* 93 (Nov. 1984): 60.
7. James Joyce, "The Dead," *Dubliners* (New York: Penguin, 1976) 196.
8. George Orwell, "Shooting an Elephant," *An Age Like This: 1920–1940,* The Collected Essays, Journalism and Letters of George Orwell, Vol. I, eds. Sonia Orwell and Ian Angus (New York: Harcourt, 1968) 241.
9. Eudora Welty, "A Worn Path," *The Collected Stories of Eudora Welty* (New York: Harcourt, 1980) 142.
10. Mario Pei, *What's in a Word?* (New York: Hawthorn Books, 1968) 20.
11. John McPhee, *Oranges* (New York: Farrar, Straus & Giroux, 1967) 64.
12. Less Thornburg, "Eyes," *International Wildlife* 13 (Sept.–Oct. 1983): 6.
13. Wanda Menke-Glückert, "For Many Germans, It's *Cool* to *Import* Words from English: *Jeans, Love,* and *Diversifikation,*" *The Chronicle of Higher Education* 18 Mar. 1987: 35.
14. "The Tuxedo: One Hundred Years of Elegance" (Special Advertising Section), *The New Yorker* 8 Sept. 1986: 76–77.
15. Stephen Jay Gould, "Sex and Size," *The Flamingo's Smile: Reflections in Natural History* (New York: Norton, 1985) 59.
16. Sam Iker, "Death from the Sky," *International Wildlife* 13 (Sept.–Oct. 1983): 46.
17. Jeff Greenfield, "The Black and White Truth about Basketball," *Esquire,* 84 (Oct. 1975): 170.
18. Pierre Szamek, "Teachers' Tests," *Harper's* 268 (Feb. 1984): 42.
19. Grace Lichtenstein, "Rocky Mountain High," *New York Times Magazine* 28 Dec. 1975: 15.
20. Jane E. Brody, *Jane Brody's Good Food Book* (New York: Norton, 1985) 5.
21. Martin Luther King, Jr., "Letter from a Birmingham Jail, April 16, 1963," *Why We Can't Wait* (New York: Harper and Row, 1963) 84–85.

22. Information from "The Cleveland Story" and "Downtown Cleveland Facts," Cleveland Growth Association, Cleveland, Ohio.
23. William R. Brown, "Why I Don't Let Students Cut My Classes," *The Chronicle of Higher Education* 28 Jan. 1987: 88.

PART II

1. Mary Robertson, "MADD Helps Crack Down on Drunk Driving," *The University Star* (Southwest Texas State University) 26 Jan. 1984: 3.
2. "Letters," *The University Star* (Southwest Texas State University) 26 Jan. 1984: 4.
3. Timothy Titcomb, *Titcomb's Letters to Young People* (New York: Scribner, Armstrong, 1875) 40.
4. Mary Wood-Allen and Sylvanus Stall, *What a Young Woman Ought to Know* (Philadelphia: Vir Publishing, 1898) 225.
5. R. J. Reynolds Tobacco Company, advertisement reprinted in Donald McQuade and Robert Atwan, eds., *Popular Writing in America,* 2nd ed. (New York: Oxford UP, 1980) 60.
6. R. J. Reynolds Tobacco Company, advertisement appearing in Money 13 (Apr. 1984): 6.
7. David A. Noebel, *Rhythm, Riots and Revolution* (Tulsa, OK: Christian Crusade Publications, 1966) 24.
8. My thanks to Elvin Holt, who supplied the material used in this exercise.
9. "Pluto," *The Concise Columbia Encyclopedia,* 1983.
10. Robert Jastrow, *Red Giants and White Dwarfs,* rev. ed. (New York: Warner Books, 1979) 154.
11. Rodnay Zaks, *The CP/M Handbook* (Berkeley, CA: Sybex, 1980) 1.
12. *An Introduction to CP/M Features and Facilities* (Pacific Grove, CA: Digital Research, 1978) 1.
13. James P. Degnan, "Masters of Babble," *Harper's* 253 (Sept. 1976): 37.
14. William Zinsser, *The Lunacy Boom* (New York: Harper and Row, 1970) 41.
15. William Zinsser, *On Writing Well,* 3rd ed. (Harper and Row, 1985) 86–87.

PART III

1. Robert Jastrow, *Red Giants and White Dwarfs,* rev. ed. (New York: Warner Books, 1979) 27–28.
2. R. J. Reynolds Tobacco Company, advertisement appearing in *Time* 19 Mar. 1984: 58.
3. Adapted from Joseph Alper, "The Stradivarius Formula," *Science 84,* 5 (Mar. 1984): 37–38.
4. Alison Lurie, *The Language of Clothes* (New York: Random House, 1981) 3.
5. Adapted from "Nestworks," *Natural History* 91 (Sept. 1982): 80–81.
6. Judith Murray, "Pumpkin beyond Pie," *Gourmet* 18 (Oct. 1983): 52.
7. "Types of Pliers," *Reader's Digest Complete Do-It-Yourself Manual* (Pleasantville, NY: Reader's Digest Association, 1973) 22.

8. Some information adapted from *Elephants* (San Diego, CA: Wildlife Education P, 1980).
9. Eudora Welty, *One Writer's Beginnings* (Cambridge, MA: Harvard UP, 1984) 14.
10. Betty Rollin, "Motherhood: Who Needs It?" *Look* 22 Sept. 1970: 15.
11. Boyce Rensberger, "In Elephant Country," *Natural History* 91 (Spet. 1982): 74.
12. Jon N. Leonard, Jack L. Hofer, and Nathan Pritikin, *Live Longer Now* (New York: Grosset & Dunlap, 1974) 8–9.
13. Adapted from "W. H. Auden," *Critical Survey of Poetry* (Englewood Cliffs, NJ: Salem P, 1983) 1: 71.
14. Ernest Hemingway, *Death in the Afternoon* (New York: Scribner's, 1960) 105.
15. Alan Devoe, *Lives Around Us* (New York: Creative Age P, 1942) 208–209.
16. Bruno Bettelheim and Karen Zelan, "Why Children Don't Like to Read," *The Atlantic* 248 (Nov, 1981): 25.
17. Reay Tannahill, *Sex in History* (New York: Stein & Day, 1980) 94.
18. William O. Douglas, *The Right of the People* (New York: Doubleday, 1958) 158.
19. William E. Leuchtenburg et al., *The Age of Change,* The Life History of the United States (New York: Time-Life Books, 1974) 12: 112–113.
20. Sing Lau, "The Effect of Smiling on Person Perception," *The Journal of Social Psychology* 117 (1982): 66.
21. Adapted from Michael Hutchins and Victoria Stevens, "Olympic Mountain Goats," *Natural History* 90 (Jan. 1981): 62, 63, 65.
22. Adapted from "Currents," *Science 84,* 5 (Mar. 1984): 10, 14.
23. Adapted from Millicent E. Selsam and Jerome Wexler, *The Amazing Dandelion* (New York: William Morrow, 1977) 5, 6, 10, 13, 42, 43, 44.
24. John F. Kennedy, Inaugural Address, January 20, 1961.
25. Aini Rajanen, *Of Finnish Ways* (Minneapolis: Dillon P, 1981) 123.
26. Malcolm Cowley, *The View from 80* (New York: Viking, 1980) 8.
27. Jerry B. Davis and Ruth B. Davis, "Teaching Mainstreamed Learning Disabled Students: Some Practical Suggestions for the Classroom Teacher," *Education* 102 (1982): 424–425.
28. Samuel Langhorne Clemens (Mark Twain), *Adventures of Huckleberry Finn* (New York: Norton, 1977) 18.
29. Tom Wolfe, *The Kandy-Kolored Tangerine-Flake Streamline Baby* (New York: Farrar, Straus & Giroux, 1965) 167.
30. Jeanette Covert Nolan, *The Story of Martha Washington* (New York: Grosset & Dunlap, 1954) 174.
31. Robert D. Hess and Kathleen A. Camara, "Post-Divorce Family Relationships as Mediating Factors in the Consequences of Divorce for Children," *Journal of Social Issues* 35 (1979): 82.
32. William Zinsser, *On Writing Well,* 3rd ed. (New York: Harper and Row, 1985) 7.
33. Loren Eiseley, *The Immense Journey* (New York: Random House, 1957) 1.
34. Eldridge Cleaver, *Soul on Ice* (New York: McGraw-Hill, 1968) 67.

PART IV

1. Adapted from "Beaver," *Encyclopaedia Britannica,* 1974, *Micropaedia.*
2. Adapted from Linda Grant De Pauw, *Founding Mothers* (Boston: Houghton Mifflin, 1975) 12–15.

3. Adapted from "Geosphere," *Geo* 4 (Oct. 1982): 118.
4. Adapted from "Geosphere," *Geo* 5 (July 1983): 106.
5. IBM advertisement appearing in *Time* 21 May 1984: 22–23.
6. Adapted from Dirk van Loon, *Small-Scale Pig Raising* (Charlotte, VT: Garden Way Publishing, 1978) 38–40.
7. Adapted from Ingeborg S. MacHaffie and Margaret A. Nielsen, *Of Danish Ways* (Minneapolis: Dillon P, 1976) 17.
8. Adapted from Fritz Müller, *The Living Arctic* (Toronto: Methuen, 1981) 79.
9. Adapted from Ken Croswell, "Stars Too Small to Burn," *Astronomy* 12 (Apr. 1984): 15.
10. Adapted from "Geosphere," *Geo* 4 (Nov. 1982): 128, 116.
11. Richard Ellis, "Killer from the Deep," *Geo* 5 (Mar. 1983): 92.
12. Adapted from Wayne Lynch, "Great Balls of Snakes," *Natural History* 92 (Apr. 1983): 65–66.
13. Henry David Thoreau, *Walden and Civil Disobedience,* ed. Sherman Paul (Boston: Houghton Mifflin, 1960) 1.
14. Lillian Hellman, *Pentimento* (Boston: Little, Brown, 1973) 265.
15. Adapted from "Cucumber," a card published by the Chas. C. Hart Seed Co., 1980.
16. Thomas Jefferson et al., The Declaration of Independence.
17. Some information adapted from David Wallechinsky, Irving Wallace, and Amy Wallace, *The Book of Lists* (New York: Bantam, 1978) 317–318.
18. Muriel Spark, *The Driver's Seat* (New York: Knopf, 1970) 109–110.
19. My thanks to Miles Wilson, who supplied material for this exercise from his unpublished novel, *Fire Season.*
20. Adapted from Alexander Petrunkevitch, "The Spider and the Wasp," *Scientific American* 187 (Aug. 1952): 22.

PART V

1. Adapted from *Reader's Digest Complete Do-It-Yourself Manual* (Pleasantville, NY: Reader's Digest Association, 1973) 160.
2. Adapted from "Geosphere," *Geo* 5 (Jan. 1983): 120.
3. Adapted from Mary Wood-Allen and Sylvanus Stall, *What a Young Woman Ought to Know* (Philadelphia: Vir Publishing, 1898) 35.
4. Adapted from Carrol B. Fleming, "Maidens of the Sea Can Be Alluring, but Sailor, Beware," *Smithsonian* 14 (June 1983): 86, 88, 89, 90, 92.
5. Adapted from Lewis Thomas, *The Lives of a Cell* (New York: Viking, 1974) 96.
6. Richard Hofstadter, *Anti-Intellectualism in American Life* (New York: Knopf, 1963) 236.
7. Eldridge Cleaver, *Soul on Ice* (New York: McGraw-Hill, 1968) 43.
8. Lewis Thomas, *The Medusa and the Snail* (New York: Viking, 1979) 126.
9. Adapted from an Epson advertisement appearing in *Science 84,* 5 (June 1984): 77.
10. Adapted from Leigh P. Beadle, *Brew It Yourself* (New York: Farrar, Straus & Giroux, 1971) 96.
11. Adapted from Delbert Clark, "What Makes a Genius?" *Saturday Review,* 12 November 1955: 9.

12. Quoted material from "Highlights," *Science 84,* 5 (April 1984): 12 [examples and items 1–3] and Barbara W. Tuchman, *A Distant Mirror* (New York: Knopf, 1978), pp. xiii, 98, 119 [items 4–7].

PART VI

1. Ramond Queneau, *Exercises in Style,* trans. Barbara Wright (New York: New Directions, 1981) 72–73.
2. Adapted from Margaret Culley, "Preface," Kate Chopin, *The Awakening,* ed. Margaret Culley (New York: Norton, 1976) vii.
3. Adapted from Stephen MacLean, "Moviemakers from Down Under," *Geo* 4 (Nov. 1982): 59, 61, 64.

PART VII

1. My thanks to Robert O'Connor, who supplied some of the material for this exercise.
2. Niels H. Lauersen, *Childbirth with Love* (New York: Putnam's, 1983) 229.

About the Author

Michael Hennessy (Ph.D., Marquette University) is Associate Professor of English at John Carroll University, where he teaches courses in composition and literature. Before moving to John Carroll, he taught at Memphis State University and at Southwest Texas State University. At Southwest Texas he directed the English department writing program for four years. His publications include *The Borzoi Practice Book for Writers* (Knopf, 1985), as well as essays and reviews on composition pedagogy and on the work of Shakespeare, Auden, and the contemporary British poet Charles Tomlinson.

Notes